What People R...

"If you find yourself just treading water waiting for life to happen, READ THIS BOOK. Find a Career That Rocks!"

-Zach Aslett

"This is a must read for students who want to go to college."

-Jake Rice

"It made me create and imagine things that I would have never done without the prompt to do so. I was eager to discover the next exercise because I found them fun to do and they helped me pinpoint certain things about the person I want to become. I always had a broad view of this person and the book helped me narrow my perception."

-Bill Baker

"For those of you who know what you want to do in life, and for those of you who have absolutely no idea, *Life in the World of Yomo* is a book that will ensure you a long-term, happy career."

-Chase Cowin

"This book is life changing and should be a freshman read for every university. It really opened my eyes to what I wanted to do with my degree and that it doesn't have to be boring!"

-Aubrey Winjum

"*Yomo* is like the rescue rope that drags you from the currents of life that have carried you away from your dreams. Grab on, shake the fear of failure and get back to being what you know you've always wanted to be."

-Forrest Moranda

"This book helped me regain my passion, not only in my career but in life! I can now create happiness for myself."
-Tassarah Weatherly

"GREAT BOOK… Fabulous exercises and insight for the future."
-Wendy Jo

"This is an amazing book! I wish this information had been available to me as a freshman in college."
-Dan Holland

"What a revolution on the way I think in day-to-day situations. I absolutely loved this book and will keep it with me as a reference that helped me find my 'key to success'."
-Samantha Telford

"After reading this book, I now miss being a kid! I aspire to never get too old to chase my dreams, and to never lose sight of what makes me happy!"
-Emily Alexander

"I recommend this book to people of all ages. Creating your Yomo takes you back to a simpler time when the hardest decision you had to make was what game to play or what picture to color. Yomo WILL change your life!"
-Lisa Romer Keele

"This book will wake you up! Expect to be activated and energized when you read about how anyone can wake up on Monday and like his or her job."
-M. Hubbard

"*Life in the World of Yomo* is a great book for anyone wanting a meaningful career. Read it and use it."
-Zach DeKruyf

"This was such a great book and I highly recommend it to people who are going to college or trying to find out who they are and what they want to do with life... This book has truly made me look at my life and career path in a different way. Thank You!"
-Bobby Prieto

"This was one of the most individualized critical thinking books I have ever read. I was working through the exercises and forgot I was working — it was a blast!"
-Heather Browne

"*Yomo* is the solution to the career blues!"
-Blake Farris

"This book totally makes it possible to get rid of the baggage that holds you back and embrace the new you; where all your dreams have been waiting... It has changed the direction of my life in looking at employment and in looking at personal change for the better."
-Jason Smart

"Find your Yomo! A whirlwind of self-evaluation that helps one a achieve success through easily achievable goals. Let your Yomo guide you and determine who you are."
-Neil Christiansen

"This book changed my perception of what a 'career' is. Let your Yomo take over and do something you are truly passionate about!"
-Kyle Takak

"*Life in the World of Yomo* is a great book for a college graduate. It is a fun read that takes you through the steps of finding out what you really want in a job."
-Shelby Baglien

"This book has helped me to realize that I can achieve happiness and success in my career and life. I always thought my dreams would only be dreams, but this book has helped me see that they my life can be a success, in every aspect."

-Coralee McCarthy

"Dr. Luke makes crazy look good!"

-Brian Lynch

"This book was such a great read with all the humor, education, and applications that the book has you complete. I strongly suggest reading it to see the personal success you can be and the help you will receive to find the perfect job that rocks!"

-Gina Barton

LIFE IN THE WORLD OF YOMO
12 STEPS TO A PERFECT CAREER

TRY IT. IT FEELS GOOD.

DR. MELISSA LUKE

Copyright © Dr. Melissa Luke, 2012

Design/layout by
Creative Factory
www.CreativeFactoryDenver.com

Published by
The Educational Publisher
www.EduPublisher.com

ISBN: 978-1-934849-94-1

Contents

How Did this Book Make it to Print?   1

Chapter 1: Introduction   5
Exercise #1: Finding My Yomo's Emotions and Qualities   14
Exercise #2: Steal Yourself Some Personality   17

Chapter 2: A Dream in Crisis   21
Exercise #3: My Yomo's Mission Statement   36

Chapter 3: Are You Standard?   39
Exercise #4: Superhero Sized Strengths   50
Exercise #5: My Exceptional Skills   52

Chapter 4: Changing Our Mind Games   53
Exercise #6: Traits to Trash   75
Exercise #7: Work My Yomo Likes   76

Chapter 5: Innovation Shapes Our World   79
Exercise #8: Invent a Career   97

Chapter 6: Gaining Focus and Being Persistent   103
Exercise #9: Family Matters   107

Chapter 7: Specialization and Entrepreneurship   111
Exercise #10: Make Money Money   127

Chapter 8: Persistence   131
Exercise #11: Foundations and Networks   137

Chapter 9: In the End, Be Happy   141

Chapter 10: Putting it All Together   157
Exercise #12: Draw Your Yomo   165
The 45-Day Challenge   167

Acknowledgments

This book is for **Krista Krantz,** (1970-1996). My fantastic college friend whose tragic death inspired me to love what I do, so that I can inspire others to love what they do while pursuing a career. Don't wait until tomorrow because nobody can guarantee it will come.

I'd also like to pay tribute to the late co-founder and CEO of Apple Inc., **Steve Jobs**, (1955-2011). A legendary innovator, who pushed himself for excellence right up to his last expiring moment of life.

"Your time is limited, so don't waste it living someone else's life. Don't be trapped by dogma — which is living with the results of other people's thinking. Don't let the noise of others' opinions drown out your own inner voice. And most important, have the courage to follow your heart and intuition. They somehow already know what you truly want to become. Everything else is secondary."

-Steve Jobs, Stanford University's
2005 Commencement Address

How Did this Book Make it to Print?

I would like to thank my old roommate and dear friend Betty Fahy for pushing me to write this book. She called me one afternoon because her dreams were focused for two solid weeks around a book that she decided I needed to write. She said people needed to hear what I had to say. I told her I was having the same thoughts but I hate to write; I love to speak. Betty told me to get a ghostwriter, learn how to use dictation software, or find someone off of Fiverr.com to do the project because she was sick of dreaming about it. Could I really get someone to write my book for $5? No. I did look though.

Betty is one of those people who can envision things in people that they can't see in themselves. She told me that she was going to personally fly to Denver and stick asparagus up my nose if I didn't start the book immediately. Knowing Betty too well, the thought terrified me — I hate asparagus.

Crazy ideas are not new to us. In our roomie days we told people that we sold European tumbleweeds for a living. We didn't have jobs, and since not having a job is apparently unacceptable, we needed a good cover. We tried acting like under cover FBI agents for a week, but nobody believed us with the exception of one toothless man residing in the Verde Valley of Arizona. We found him in a western saloon and informed him we were tracking a villain. He was visibly scared of us, but I also think he was a little drunk. Acting as salesmen for dead shrubbery was easier to pull off, but after selling one

European tumbleweed for $75, which we found in the Arizona desert, we closed shop. Tumbleweeds are hard to catch when it's windy.

We followed our whims from one crazy idea to another in search of jobs that didn't feel like work. In fact, having jobs that don't feel like work has always been my life goal. Anyway, after the success of our tumbleweed business, we decided to take our capital and look into building pyramids. We jumped in the car and drove to Palm Springs to scout a location for our first archeological, architectural endeavor. We learned we would need millions of dollars to build our project, which we did not have. We did, however, have Delta airline miles. After purchasing a $12 box of wine, we called the airline to secure flights to Greece. We didn't know why, but it seemed like a good idea at the time. Willy, a good friend of ours, stopped by during our attempt to book our next adventure. He said, "Ladies, you can't just buy a box of wine, and fly to Greece. You need to get jobs." We didn't go, but only because we were short 10,000 miles to buy the tickets.

Distraught with life in general, we purchased a gallon of pumpkin ice cream, got two plastic spoons, and sat at a bus stop with the box of wine to think about our careers. Everything seemed so utterly boring in the world of work. The new plan was to jump on the next bus that came along. It didn't matter the destination, we just wanted to get away. Lucky for us, no buses ever came.

We both eventually found careers that we respectively loved. Betty was right. I needed to write a book on how we got to the place where we could love our jobs. I began to write, but I needed help with the process so I called in the "big dogs."

How Did this Book Make it to Print? 3

The first step was backing up my notions with concrete data. My great friend Everett Meyers, a Professor of International Finance and Economics at New York University, assisted me in this. I have been stealing his work for a decade. His research in the doctoral program at NYU on The Success Returns for Graduates of 4-year, for-profit, Postsecondary Institutions came in very handy. Note: Ev, I may have stolen some data from your doctoral dissertation for this book and probably forgot to cite you. So, I figured I would just reference it here. We're still good right?

Second, turning creativity and thoughts into ideas, careers, and books can't be successfully accomplished without a mentor and I have one of the best. Loch Anderson, co-founder and principal of Foushee and Associates in Bellevue, WA pushed me to stay on track and never lose sight of my vision. I admire his business sense and assistance with my projects, but even more he is a fabulous friend that I aspire to beat when racing anything with wheels (on a race track, of course). We all know this will never happen, but I'm just going to put it out there.

Third, my friends and family, (many of whom think that I am far more talented than I personally believe myself to be), were a huge part of this project. They have always been supportive of everything I do in life. They push me to accomplish great things. I don't want to disappoint or ruin their grandiose perspectives of what I am capable of accomplishing, so I try harder everyday to succeed because of them.

However, the most important person on this project was my sister Margaret Luke. If I could figure out how to sell her brilliance and talent in a can, I would be a billionaire.

She has made me feel like anything is possible and she is everything I am not. Anything I have accomplished in life has fingerprints of her genius on the plan, including this one. Years ago she teasingly told me she was a witch. Initially, I thought this was funny, but I think she may be right. She's like Glenda the Good Witch from the *Wizard of Oz* (without the pink dress and wand). My sister really does help dreams come true. I'm just happy no brooms were involved.

Lastly, I would like to thank *Fast Company* for making a fantastic magazine, which identifies the great innovators of our time. The magazine has given me inspiration and motivates me on a monthly basis to create positive changes for our society. Hopefully we will meet soon. I intend to be on your cover someday.

It's funny how inspiration from great people can help another person accomplish almost anything in life. Add a touch of desire to succeed in the world as a great innovator, and you have the magic formula. Substitute your personal inspirations, your motivators, and your desires and it will work for you if you allow it to. I'm going to take you to a magical land called YomoWorld: A place where perfect careers really do come true. No bus stops required.

If you like to experiment then you are in the right place.

Chapter 1: Introduction

Yomo: A visual manifestation of everything you want to be in your personal and professional life that will guide changes in your brain to help you achieve your dreams.

YomoWorld: A place that connects highly innovative businesses and cool start-up companies with the right people.

"The greatest discovery of my generation is that human beings can alter their lives by altering their attitudes and minds… If you change your mind you change your life."

-William James

People often ask me why I never seem to have a job, and yet live like the queen of some spectacular country. They also want to know why I am contagiously happy a great deal of my waking hours. I explain, "That's how I made my brain work." I feel the same anxiety about what I am going to do with the rest of my life at the age of 40 as I did at the age of 20. The only difference is that I am old enough to know this feeling of anxiety is normal. I then explain that I am an entrepreneur, and we entrepreneurs are *always* working, even though we are often hopping from one fantastic idea to another. We are, I guess, the manifestation of the infamous reply of the French Philosopher Rene Descartes: "Cogito ergo sum" or "I think therefore I am." For some reason, however, this response does not quench the thirst of my students or acquaintances. They want to know more; they want to learn how to innovate, develop, and build ideas like I do. They want to know how to work in their respective "field of dreams." I, on the other hand, wonder why people sit in traffic everyday like ants in a plastic ant farm to get to work five or more days a week, where they labor excessive hours at jobs they hate. It sounds horrible. I would rather string toilet paper between my toes and light it on fire than sit in a cubicle with fluorescent lighting all day, everyday.

When I started writing this book, I wanted it to be a guide to help 18 to 24-year-olds who have graduated from high school or college find a fantastic and innovative career they would love for many years. I also wanted to prepare Generation Y with a realistic expectation of what the professional world is really like and the kinds of sacrifices they will be expected to make in the name of the almighty dollar. However, during my research, I learned most adults over the age of 30 don't like their respective careers. The work world is getting more and more grim with each passing day. Studies by The Conference Board and CareerBuilder.com in 2010 show that over 80 percent of people in the United States dislike their current career and job satisfaction is at its lowest in two decades. Unfortunately, most employers take great pride in locking employees in cubicles for long periods of time and refuse to create a work environment that is enjoyable for anyone. In order to change attitudes towards work, it has to start with the organizations themselves.

However, getting most employers to try anything new requires a lot of outside pressure. Change, on every level, begins with the individual. It begins with the new wave of employees who are entering the workforce. It involves changing the mindset of people who have been on the job for years. It requires an open mind filled with non-standard thinking.

What's Going on Inside...

Over the past decade I have worked with thousands of students who were passionate about their fields of study. While they were all interested in something a little bit different, they all seemed to have one goal in mind: Get a degree. Their logic was "I'll get a degree to have a better life." According to the 2011 U.S. Census Bureau, Statistical Abstract of the United States on Education, a degree means higher pay; to most of us this means nicer things and financial security.

Isn't that why so many people have gone to college in America? To get a job that pays better so they can have a more satisfying life? If that is the case, then why do 80 percent of working adults hate their jobs? What happened?

As part of my research for this book, I surveyed thousands of people who are dissatisfied with their jobs. I wanted to know why a person would do something everyday that made him or her miserable. I wanted to know what was different about people who loved their jobs and people who despised their jobs. Too many folks are waking up in the morning and taking a sip of cyanide for no other reason than everyone else is doing it. Who started this cult?

I feel one of the biggest reasons people are comfortable being unhappy in their careers is something called "group think." If a grand majority of society hates going to work everyday, then it seems fair to be in the "norm" and feel the same way. Dissatisfaction in numbers leads to accepted mediocrity.

In *Man's Search for Meaning,* author Victor Frankl says that in psychiatry there is a condition called the "delusion of reprieve." In this condition prisoners get the illusion that they will be reprieved right before death. In our working lives, I would say we have a "delusion of acceptance." We think our lives are in a permanent state of compromise and the outcome is out of our control. We believe we cannot alter this state but magically the circumstances will get better. We also call this "wishful thinking." Have you become a prisoner of your own career?

A recent study reported that 67 percent of college graduates from the 2010 graduating class have yet to acquire a full time job six months after graduation. Are the jobs not available? Or are the available jobs so boring that Gen Y refuses to accept them? I recently trained a large company in Dallas, TX, which had over 500 employees that were unhappy. I learned that the company had implemented a daily activities tracking system for the customer service employees, down to clocking their bathroom breaks. Who wants that? A person can't tinkle in peace? Jason Dorsey, also known as the "Gen-Y Guy" states the current workforce between the ages of 20 and 27 stays with an employer for an average of 13 months before moving on. That is a little different from Baby Boomers (55 to 64) who, according to a January 2010 U.S. Bureau of Labor Statistics report, averaged 10 years in a job. To be honest, after spending years training inside corporate America, I wouldn't want to work for most of the companies I have examined. I'm surprised Gen Y sticks around for 13 months. I would have left most of these places on the first day. Generation Z will probably stay in a normal corporate job for 13 minutes. They probably won't even make it past signing the required tax forms unless someone makes a mobile application for them.

Is This a Global Issue?

No, I don't think so. On a recent trip to Europe I spent many days questioning people about their careers. Yes, I am that annoying traveler who will talk to absolutely anyone on planes, trains, and in elevators, and restrooms, and pubs. When I go through immigration and customs, I think I ask them more questions than they ask me. I didn't poll enough people to calculate any proper statistics, but in general I firmly believe Europeans are happier with their careers compared to Americans. Could this be partially due to the amount of vacation days Europeans take in a given year compared to what's normal here? The average number of annual vacation days in the United States is 13 compared to 38 days per year in France. Would an extra 25 days of vacation a year make you happier? Maybe not. Something else is contributing to this job dissatisfaction.

From what I can determine, the mindset of the European people is completely different. The Italians nap, work a bit, sleep, work a bit, drink wine, work a little bit, eat, work a little bit, and a few other things I can't add here... Then, work a bit. The Dutch are the same; life is easy if you make it as such. Is it normal to have a Haunted House in December? It is in Amsterdam, because it's fun.

People in the UK may be a tad more serious than the Italians, but it is rare to hear of a person dreading their career. I know a few exist but I couldn't find any of them. The bartenders are content with their jobs and most of the time they don't even get tips. What do the Europeans know that we don't? I'm going to go out on a limb here and say it's their grander, positive mentality. Europeans know their talents and figure out how to use them well. They don't complain as much as we do; they simply make things happen and are content with what they have.

What many have known as the "American Dream" has turned into a nightmare. We need to go back to the basics and figure out what makes us happy. Just ask the well-rested Italians.

Something is broken, and it is the link between corporate America and the people placing themselves in these unfulfilling jobs. It is my goal to help people think in a different direction in order to get a job that rocks. The current plan is: Get a degree, spin a resume, and get a job. I am here to offer more steps to that plan and offer a new set of questions to ask yourself when approaching the inevitable question: "What am I going to do with my life today?"

Would you believe me if I told you multi-millionaires are paying students to start their own companies if they drop out of college? If I offered you $100,000 to build a new idea, concept or product, would you drop out of school to do it? Peter Thiel, co-founder of PayPal, is doing exactly this. Dozens of highly intelligent students from excellent schools such as Purdue and Princeton walked out the door of academia to try something new. They don't want to be stuck in some of the stale jobs corporate America has to offer.

I have told thousands of people to leave their careers or their universities over the past decade. The responses range from "Are you flipping nuts?" to "Why the heck not?" In fact, I have even been told that my thoughts on careers are irrational and aggravating to some people. You may very well be one of those people. However, I dare you to knock on wood if any of these statements ring a bell:

I Can't Leave My Job Because...

- I won't be able to pay my mortgage, car payment, bills, etc. (Who bought the house, car, and made credit card charges? Who can get rid of all the above as well? Hint: Not me.)
- I don't have any other talents or experience. (How strange. The only thing you know how to do is something you don't like? Sounds like a voodoo hex.)
- I have a family and they rely on my income. (Your family depends on you to model for them a state of happiness; not misery. If not, why would you bring them into this world to begin with?)
- The economy is bad and I can't switch careers; I'm lucky to have a job at all... (No, you're lucky to be alive. You are cursed if you think good fortune is having a bad job.)

The truly interesting portion of my research was this: When I asked people if they could become what they wanted to be when they were nine years old, today, would they do so? The answer was a resounding "Yes."

Now let me ask you this, think back to the day you first looked your parents or best friend in the eye, and said "I'm going to be a (fill in the blank) when I grow up."

Are you doing what you said you would? If not, what happened to you? If someone handed you a magic wish ball, would you make your nine-year-old self's dreams come true? If so, you're reading the right book. Oddly enough, my first business endeavor happened to be selling dreams, and as luck would have it most of mine have come true. I am here to help reprogram the good parts of your brain back to adolescence in search of your dream career to help you make it a reality. Even if you don't want to be what you wanted to be 10 or 20 years ago, one of the critical components to success is you must start thinking like a child again.

Most successful innovators, entrepreneurs, and talented business people share this simple truth: They lack standardization of thought. They know how to find something they want and learn how to acquire it through thinking in a childlike state. People who are happy with their careers, even the richest businessmen, typically don't care about money, and they absolutely don't have standard thoughts that justify staying in a bad place just because of the income. If you love your big house and fancy car, but hate your career, you may very well be an idiot. We can fix this. People who are happy in their careers are not standard; there are fewer than 20 percent of them in the United States. It is my goal to help you become non-standard. After applying the concepts outlined in this book, I can't promise that your friends and family members will think you're sane, but I can guarantee you will be happy, or at the bare minimum on your way to becoming successful in your own right.

Over the course of this book, I will prepare you to hunt for a job that has *meaning*. I'm not going to spend chapters and valuable page space discussing winning interview techniques, how to properly format your resume, or how to make your online profile standout. I don't think these methods work the way we want them to. While the online arena has changed the way people search for jobs, there's yet to be a protocol that is effective at matching talented job hunters with jobs they actually like.

This necessary and inevitable change all starts with a shift in our thinking. Every job interviewer I've ever met smiles and nods with approval whenever a candidate says anything about "thinking outside the box." Now is the time to actually do it. Thinking outside of the box and changing the way people view their jobs, employment, and career satisfaction is the inspiration behind the career-building concept I call "Yomo."

We all have a Yomo. Currently, your Yomo is a nameless, shapeless blob that is just sitting there waiting for you to come along and put life into it. As we progress through the book, the Yomo will start to take shape, and by the last chapter, the Yomo will embody the very essence of what you hope to become in your life and in your career.

Typically, we avoid engaging in an experience that we are fearful of because we have no prior experience with the situation. In other words, we don't have any recall of the experience, so it is unknown and uncomfortable. We do not experience anything in the world that is new, such as a new career, without some relative fear. However, we displace this fear when building a Yomo, because in our minds, the Yomo has nothing to lose, and we can't feel rejected or embarrassed if it does something wrong. Knowledge and experience removes the sense of fear. Our Yomos encounter the experience first to dispel the fear in our mind. When you become your Yomo, your fears have already been dealt with.

The Yomo is everything you wanted to be but didn't have the time/money/guts to become. It will serve as a beacon to the career you truly aspire to have. If you put everything you truly want to accomplish into your

Yomo, then it will serve as a constant, daily reminder of everything you have ever wanted to become. At first, the idea of the Yomo will seem like a pretty foreign concept. However, throughout this book I'll guide you through several activities to help you develop your Yomo. In the final exercise, you will construct your Yomo and gain insight on how to use it to gain the career and livelihood you've always wanted.

For now, let's stop with the five-year-plans and the constant retouching of our resume. We need to stop assuming that our dream job will be waiting for us somewhere down the line, several years away. Let's stop making excuses as to why we haven't done what we've always wanted to do. For the rest of this book you will live in the world of Yomo. Let's focus on what we want to do *today*.

Close your eyes, click your heals together three times, and repeat after me: "There is no place like (fill in the blank)." Forget *home*, going back to that place may land you in the middle of a bunch of flying monkeys. It's not necessarily a good place to be.

Exercise #1: Finding My Yomo's Emotions and Qualities

Think back to one of your fondest memories about yourself before the age of 12. Revisit that memory, and identify all of your emotions and your elated feelings. Yomos do not have DNA, so we don't want to inject yours into the avatar; however we do want to add any elated feelings you have had in your life before the age of 12. After the age of 12, in most people, conscious awareness begins and there is a significant activity increase in the neocortex (the part of the brain that is involved in higher functions such as sensory perception, coordination, spatial reasoning, conscious thought, and language). We want to go back to those thoughts you had as a child, when "No" and "It can't be done" were not a part of your understanding.

I want you to describe your fondest memory and any associated feelings on the following page.

Here's my personal example: In 5th grade, I would buy five candy bars for a dollar. I would then bring them to school and sell them to my friends for 50 cents a piece, making a fairly hefty profit. I felt powerful because I owned my own business, smart because nobody else had thought of this, and financially savvy because I had more money than anyone else at school. My intent was to buy a horse (more on that story later). I was a mini Donald Trump in grade school, but with better hair.

My Yomo is:
Powerful
Smart
Rich
Dedicated

Your turn. Identify the feelings and qualities you are most proud of from your fondest memory and list them on the next page. Lock them into your current thoughts so they are as vivid as hearing the crunch of an apple after taking a bite (you probably did not need to find an apple and eat it to know that sound, feeling, taste, and emotion connected to that bite). Before you move to the next step, try to retrieve these feelings at least 24 times in the next 24 hours.

Life in the World of Yomo: 12 Steps to a Perfect Career

Your fondest memory about yourself:

Any emotions or qualities tied to this memory:

Exercise #2: Steal Yourself Some Personality

Personality is something we develop over time. Our failures and successes, adventures and challenges make us who we are. But so do the people we associate with and the people we are attracted to.

Fortunately, stealing personalities is not a crime (unlike identity theft), so make a list of people you like, people whose personalities you are attracted to. Next to each of those names, write down the things about that person you love the most. If you were to adopt personality traits or habits from that person, what would they be and why?

My example: In high school, one of my neighbors was nicknamed Moles. Moles was very popular and well liked by everyone. However, I was not. I had just moved to a new school and was considered an "outsider." She was in the "popular crowd," which I was not for some reason and they took particular interest in being very mean to me on a daily basis. Moles befriended me and soon became my best friend despite what others thought. She was not concerned with her "status." Moles graduated, married the love of her life, Joe, opened her own salon in Scottsdale, Arizona, and they now have four beautiful children. To this day Moles has the fantastic personality of a 12-year-old child and is always laughing, playing jokes on people, smiling, and going so far out of her way to make others happy that she makes Mother Theresa look like a crook. She is extremely smart and talented, but it is her childlike personality and passion that makes people automatically aspire to be better. She has her trials and tribulations like the rest of us, but she manages to make them insignificant while double dog daring you to eat a plate of jalapeño peppers. Moles makes any day enjoyable and I honestly see the world bathed in a different light when I am around her, even 25 years later.

My Yomo takes these qualities from Moles:
Lovable
Joyful
Fun
Non-judgmental
Childlike
Considerate

Now list the people you admire, detailing their most desirable traits below:

Over the next 24 hours try to respond to situations the way each of the people you listed would. Use the traits they have rather than your own. For example, I might get angry; Moles would just ask someone to eat an apple that tastes terrible, and then laugh the minute their face puckered.

Chapter 2: A Dream in Crisis

"Here's to the crazy ones. The misfits. The rebels. The troublemakers. The round pegs in the square holes. The ones who see things differently. They're not fond of rules, and they have no respect for the status quo. You can quote them, disagree with them, glorify, or vilify them. But the only thing you can't do is ignore them. Because they change things. They push the human race forward. And while some may see them as the crazy ones, we see genius. Because the people who are crazy enough to think they can change the world, are the ones who do."

-Apple's "Think Different" Campaign

Krista Krantz, one of my best friends, made my college experience lively through her endless practical jokes. She was witty, flippant, hysterically funny and her sense of humor pushed way past the line of political correctness. She was the Jerry Seinfeld of our apartment complex. Her ability to shock was topped only by her ambition. She aspired to become a lawyer who lobbied for political and social change on Capitol Hill in Washington D.C.

Her academic record was fantastic, I think she had close to a 4.0 GPA, far better than mine (I majored in happy hour, and mastered the concept). Krista and her smarty-pants personality was truly an inspiration to everyone around us. After Krista turned 23, she started to feel a bit under the weather. A month and a few trips to the doctor later, Krista was diagnosed with cancer in her liver. Despite all treatment, the cancer then spread to her ribs, breast, and brain. Even through her numerous hospital visits and endless treatments, Krista managed to keep her spirits high and her jokes sharp – something I doubt any of us could manage if we had been in her position.

Krista's prognosis never improved, and she died at the age of 26.

A truth about this life is that no matter how fantastic or horrible we make it out to be, we all die. No one really knows when we will die, and the process seems unfair at Krista's young age, but it's a part of the game plan for everyone. We all knew that Krista would accomplish a great many things.

Then, she didn't.

Krista's tragic story serves as an inspiration to me, as I hope it does all of you: Life is mercilessly short, even if we are able to live 100 years. We all get exactly one go at it, so why bother wasting time doing jobs we don't like?

While Krista was undergoing treatments, I was working a job as a trust account manager with a mortgage company in Arizona. I hated every day of that job, and as a result, I wasn't even doing my job right. But I didn't care. I fantasized about building a margarita machine under my desk just to make my job more interesting. What Krista seemed to understand at the time, that I was only just learning, is that this life we lead is incredibly finite. Things just happen, and the next thing you know, game over. I resolved that I wouldn't live that way anymore.

When Krista died we all had a party to celebrate her life. The next day I flew home to Arizona and quit my job. I told my boss that I had no intention of doing any sort of work that didn't make me happy. He then asked if I would stay long enough to train a new employee on how to do my job. I had to tell them that I wasn't even able to do the job correctly, and I shouldn't waste anyone's time in teaching them how to do it wrong. They still paid me to stay.

I walked out two weeks later, and every job since then has been an investment in my own happiness. I found that I am generally happier if I take jobs where I don't have a lot of upward responsibility towards supervisors. Since Krista's death, I have worked to make sure everything I do has a lasting, positive impression on those I come in contact with.

I tell you Krista's story because I don't want it to take another person's dying for you to realize that you have a limited time on this planet and you only get one chance at this life. What are you going to do with this opportunity? Can you confidently say that you would enjoy staying another day, week, or month at your current job?

How Did We Get Here?

We begin our formal educational years learning the basics: reading, writing, and arithmetic. I suppose this is a logical starting point, but it didn't make a lot of sense to me when I was a kid, and it still doesn't now. As a university professor, I see problems within the school system that hinder the pursuit of success. We don't train our youth to pursue and develop their talents; we educate them to be "well-rounded." Some of the most talented people in the world never passed the 6th grade, and a handful never stepped foot in a school at all. Steve Jobs and Bill Gates both attended school to learn something of value; when they grasped what fascinated them, they both fled to the market, driven by their passion to grow an idea. How did they each accomplish such notable careers without finishing college? The answer is simple: Both lacked standard thought. They both understood that the only way to success is to passionately follow a dream. They also hold an incredible amount of "risk taking" tolerance.

We learn at a very young age to work hard to improve upon our weaknesses. That makes no sense. I was terrible at algebra in school, so I was required to stay after school to get better at my nemesis. I still hate algebra and quite frankly don't think I have used it once in my career. I pay someone else to do what I hate but cannot avoid. Working hard at something I hate has not made me, or anyone, happy, and rarely makes people rich. Who really cares if one to the power of one equals one? If I had invented algebra, I would have at least made the answer a little more interesting, such as it would equal a cat or at a bare minimum a glass of wine so it would be useful.

Neuroscientists say that our brains do not fully develop until the age of 25. This would explain a lot of the stupid things I did in my teens and early twenties, but I still need an excuse for what I did yesterday and will probably do tomorrow. Point being, most students who go to college start at the age of 18. They are supposed to select a major and determine what they are going to do for the rest of their lives before their brain has finished maturing. That's like asking a baby to change its own diaper. An infant doesn't have the neurological development put into place to rip off a diaper, clean up the mess, and tape a new one back on. Not having a fully developed brain does not mean we are incapable of making an important decision. "Yomo" decisions must be driven by passion. We need to train our brain to think in a non-standard way.

Most traditional undergraduate students between the ages of 18 to 21 have yet to build a neurological system to know what they want to do for a career for the next 50 years. Often they feel forced to decide and later become upset because they feel as though they have made the wrong decision. If you are an 18 to 21-year-old student, don't be too concerned about your degree selection. It really doesn't matter in terms of your career. You will learn how to change that diaper later.

Sir Ken Robinson is a world-renowned thinker and author in the field of creativity in learning. In his book *The Element*, he states: "We are educating the creativity out of students." Just think. What if we had courses every year from the age of six forward, training us to follow our passion? I would not choose to dissect a dead frog, that's just gross. But, Hannibal Lecter probably would enjoy the course. Some people are happier and better at playing the violin than doing quadratic equations. Why are we wasting our time pushing subjects on our youth that they will never master? I'm not saying we need to throw the basic fundamentals out the door, but change needs to occur. The entire educational process is devaluing innovation and creativity in mankind.

To make matters worse, we don't know what to teach our youth in preparation for a career in the next decade, much less the rest of their lives. Nobody knows what the future will bring. By the year 2020, we will probably be flying around in the air like the Jetson's and banner ads will be projected on our foreheads. Yes folks, you might be able to lease your head as a billboard for extra bucks. By the year 2030, we may be living in a complete world of gamafication online as avatars that never leave home. Our business dealings will all be conducted in a make believe world for points. Forget gold and silver. The new universal currency is going to be points. Now what school offers that class for business majors? I might add this into my course next semester just to be cool.

The academic community may disagree with me on what I am about to state, and that's fine. I don't consider myself an academic even though I am one on paper: We need to stop the standardization process in our educational systems and help our children develop their true talents. In my opinion, this is why we, as individuals, rarely acquire our "dream careers." As a society we refuse to train our youth how to discover their dreams, let alone accomplish the important task of following them. How can a system that lacks innovation itself teach students to be innovative and creative?

Before you start questioning my intent, let me state that I am not trying to get you to drop out of school if you are currently attending. That's not the point, and quite frankly, I would not have a job if you all left tomorrow. At a TED (Technology, Entertainment, Design) Conference in Monterey, California in 2006, Sir Ken Robinson informed us that in the next 30 years we will have as many college graduates world wide as we have in total to date in the history of the world. Furthermore, India currently produces approximately 2.5 million graduates per year with over seventy nine thousand MBA's alone.[1] Guess what that means? An undergraduate degree will be deflated and will become the new high school diploma. I guess I don't have to worry about job retention as long as I stay a professor. What does this mean for you though? How are you going to differentiate yourself among the masses? How will an HR director find your resume more appealing than the 52,000 other applicants

---

[1] Source: Company called Brickwork (division of B2K) started by Vivek Kulkarni in India. Found in the book *The Word is Flat* by Thomas Friedman

with the same degree? The answer: you are going to have to start thinking exclusively in an area that makes you passionate.

Unemployment is at a record high; however companies are complaining they can't find the right talent. Specialization is critical. What makes you better/happier? In all honesty, you MUST love what you do or you can't shine.

What Happened to Us?

In grade school we are told that we can be whatever we want to be. Somewhere along the way, for whatever reason, this became less and less true. What we wanted to be when we were younger is replaced by the need to earn money and develop a "respectable" career. Pretty soon, we completely forget about our childhood dreams or the ambitions we had as young adults. We become office workers, we work for someone else, and our career becomes helping someone above us achieve their dreams and goals. Does anyone actually grow up to do what he or she has always wanted to do?

Sadly, not often enough. The rates of people who are unsatisfied with their job are staggering, even depressing. Few seem to have any idea how to follow a dream. More and more people today are settling into the mainstream, meeting standards, accepting trends, making ends meet, and eventually dying off. Additionally, I think that a great majority of the people who like what they do end up hating their careers because of the other miserable people around them and archaic work structures. The job in and of itself is fine but unhappy people in a gloomy organization can make a glass of champagne look like mud.

Thankfully, this cycle of thinking may soon be coming

to a close. I have been interacting with, and researching, a generation of students and young employees who are set to blow the top off everything we have come to know about living, working, and having a job, career, or livelihood. They may be the first generation of workers who genuinely love what they do for a living. Yes, they are here and they are ready to take over. I would like to introduce you to...

Generation Y (the Millennials)

For the past nine years, I have been teaching at the university level, and during that time, I have taught and mentored thousands of students. I love working with young minds. It gives me hope and optimism for our future no matter what the current economic or cultural climate may be. I especially love working with this particular group of students because I love being face to face with Generation Y.

Generation Y is the generation of people who were born in the 1980s and 1990s. This was an odd time in American history where popular culture expanded through the rise of shopping malls and MTV. The Internet was starting to become well known and used. At the same time civic organizations were promoting programs that focused on protecting children and building strong family values. Teachers were charged with the task of telling their students they could grow up to be anything they wanted to be. This is the generation who believes they all can fulfill all their dreams, and everything they do needs to focus on this.

As a result the Millennials have flooded employment offices, education centers, and job fairs looking for an opportunity to become happy, successful and change the world. They are bright-eyed and eager to make business more environmentally and socially conscious, more efficient, and more fun. They are ready to earn a living, so long as they aren't bored while they do it. They are ready to show every hiring manager and human resource officer that they are not only the right person for the job, but that they will be the key to the company's future.

While you would think that most employers would embrace ambitious and eager workers ready to make business more efficient and relevant, like the Millennials, most companies seem to be flat out afraid of them. It's common for employees who stick around with one company long enough to believe the next generation of employees will be lazy and stupid. I can tell you first hand that is not the case with Millennials. Those same long-term employees also fear new employees because they invite change. However, in today's economic climate, if a company wants to keep up with their customers and clients, change needs to happen.

Stale and stagnant workplaces are inhibiting the impact GenY is destined to make. We are boring them to death. We are lucky that the next generation of workers wants to experiment and change the way things are done in the workplace. Chances are they will make work exciting again. And when people are excited about their work, they produce better results.

However, if today's employers keep rejecting the Millennials, then we may never see this bright future workplace. If we aren't able to accept their new ideas and work styles, then the potential of the Millennials may never see the light of day, and their talent will never be put to good use. We have to keep this from happening. Part of it is up to the employer. The other part is up to the Millennials. Put your wagers up. I'm betting on the Millennials to win. If companies refuse to change, then Millennials need to start building new ones.

If the Millennials want to protect their dreams and see them come true, then they can never back down, surrender, or become "one of the crowd." They have to cut their own individual paths, which is exactly what this book is about.

Today's Millennials are graduating from college into what is being construed as a bleak employment landscape. Job growth has slowed. Companies are closing or laying off employees in record numbers and not hiring the under experienced, overly experienced, or anyone who has been unemployed for more than six months. There is very little for someone who seeks an entry-level job to be optimistic about. People are taking up jobs that don't suit them so they can pay back creditors for stuff they didn't need. Wouldn't having an awesome job that stimulates you but pays a little less be better than one you hate and leads you into a cycle of retail therapy and credit card debt? While earning more money may make an unsatisfying job more bearable, it is a well-known truth that money can't fix everything. Peer pressure and competition with the Jones's have led people to confuse what they want with what they need. People who are holding down the jobs they don't like are keeping others who would enjoy those jobs from taking their place.

If money can't buy happiness, then how are we to remain happy? Have we forgotten how to have a full and happy life without needing to rely on money? Why are we taking jobs we don't like? Furthermore, why are we staying with them long after the novelty has worn off?

The reasons are astounding. Some employees have developed a sense of learned helplessness in which they assume that every other job out there must be just as bad as their current one, so why bother looking? Or they assume that they are nowhere near quailed or able to get their shoe in the right door to obtain the job they want. They have given up on looking for something better not because they don't believe there is a better job out there, but because they have taught themselves that work in itself should be unsatisfying.

Other employees I have talked to claimed their debt is too big for them to move around careers and jobs. According to the Federal Reserve, the average American household carries an average of $8,700 in credit card debt, and in 2008, 4.79 percent of credit card accounts were considered delinquent on payment. The sad fact is, with today's interest rates, some people will never get out of the debt they have built up no matter what job they have. So, why not have a job you like?

There are those few employees out there who like their huge paychecks, but hate the job that comes with them. If they were to give up that paycheck their lavish lifestyles would go with it. These are the employees who have learned that lots of money means lots of toys means lots of happiness. Personally, I have been in their position, but I can attest that the wealthy lifestyle can result in extreme boredom.

…And boredom does funny things to people.

The first time I was rich, having too much money and spare time, I flew one of my best college friends to Seattle for the weekend to make prank phone calls. We bought a recording device and decided that we would be the next "Jerky Boys" (look them up). I called a Casino on an Indian reservation and requested to speak to the head pit boss. The phone receptionist declined my request. I then told her that he owed me $400,000 and I would cut all his fingers off if he did not pay me in 24 hours. I was transferred quickly.

Once he answered the phone we both realized that this wasn't very funny and we hung up. My friend caught the next flight back home to Connecticut, and I moved to Canada for a month. We weren't certain if the casino could track the call. We both had fears of the mafia chasing us. Who does this stuff? Bored millionaires.

I typically ask people who are working in a job they don't like: What is your happiness worth? How much does a company have to pay you to do something that makes you unhappy day in and day out? $35,000 a year? $100,000 a year? If you hate your job but keep coming back for the promise of a paycheck, then that's how much your happiness is worth to you.

What we do in our life creates our identity – the fabric of who we are. Scientists are finding genetics play a smaller part of your personality than most people think. If you spend your life doing something that is against your identity, or even the identity you wish you had, a conflict is going to develop in your psyche – at your very core. Your happiness will suffer, as will your mental and physical health, your relationships, and your ability to effectively do your job. Wouldn't it be great to think of your happiness as invaluable? Wouldn't you like to say that there is no imaginable amount of money that you would trade for your happiness? If you want to be happy with your career and your life, then you must first remove the price tag you have put on your well-being.

Adults frequently ask high school and college students one question: "What are you going to do with your life?" Isn't it an odd question? To some, that question may be borderline offensive. Your parents and your grandparents pretty much want to know how you are going to earn a living. "What are you going to do with your life?" is a question that should not have anything to do with employment or how much you earn, but when it is asked your livelihood and wealth are immediately tied together.

Why not take that question back? Instead of being asked, "What are you going to do with your life" why not ask, "What do I want to do with my life right now?" By turning the question around and asking it of yourself, you are no longer limiting the scope of the question to answers of employment. Instead, you will be thinking about the value of your time and what you need to do to make the best of it.

"What do I want to do with my life right now?" The answer to this question is the foundation to what you are going to build with the rest of this book. It will be the root of your mission statement; it will be the skeleton of your Yomo. It will, in the end, become you.

Creating a Solution

Right now I want you to start thinking more positively. I want you to all change your questions from "What can I do for money?" to "What do I want to do with my life?" Then, think infinitely. It is time to stop playing by the rules. It is time to look at the current landscape of jobs and employment as an opportunity for change, rather than the tragedy it has been made out to be. In fact, some of the most successful companies began as start-ups in the worst economic times in history. A bad economy equates to great OPPORTUNITY. It's time to have fun and follow ideas that interest you. Think experimentation and innovation.

The Chia Pet was created in the 1970s during a bad recession. Interest rates were ridiculously high, and the housing market was terrible. But people found a way to come up with spare change to buy ceramic pigs that grew weeds out their rear ends. Talk about retail therapy. I guess if you couldn't pay your mortgage, buying a Chia Pet made things better. So, who's to say you can't start selling the free pigeons strutting around your neighborhood as "outdoor bird pets?" Your business could make people happy; rather than thinking of the birds as a nuisance, they might make good pets. This is the opposite of what we learn in our economics class, but we might be able to prove the professors wrong in this case. The point is, now is the time to take whatever dream you have that you might have been told is outrageous, and do it.

It is time to inspire yourself and those around you. I want everyone to be a part of the movement of people who actually enjoy their jobs. I want everyone to strive for change. Are you all right with the way things are? Or are you ready to change things right now?

If the answer is the latter, I challenge you to start...

Reclaiming Your Dreams

Maybe you have had the same dream in mind since you were a kid. Maybe you just realized your new dream after a bad day at work. Maybe the problem is that you don't know what your dream is. This book is designed to identify your dreams and turn each one into a reality.

As I will tell you several times during the course of

this book, there is only one way to create change: from the inside. I will discuss in a later chapter how this happens on a neurological level, but to take the first step to change, you must first create a resolution to change the way you do things. Establishing a personal mission statement does this best.

Most companies write some form of mission statement to keep their business on track over the years. It is not as specific as their employee guidebook, but it is concise enough to help them make the right choice on difficult decisions. Personal mission statements are very similar. The statement may not be enough to dictate everything that happens in your day, but it will serve as a guide to help you keep to your long-term goals. It will help you to start to think beyond the way school has trained you to think or the goals your parents set for you. A mission statement is a way for you to get whatever it is YOU genuinely want.

Some of the finest leaders throughout history have maintained their focus and made their wildest dreams come true by first writing them down. Think Martin Luther King Jr. Once you start to see your name next to the things you want, your mind will start to process these seemingly wild ambitions as something real. You will discover that reality becomes what you think about constantly, and vice versa. Dr. King had a dream, and I personally think he had a plan to make it come to fruition.

Determine today if you plan to change your current path. If the answer is "No," return this book and stop complaining about your life. Nobody wants to hear about your misery. Flip to page 142 of the phone book and see if you find any enlightenment there.

If the answer is "Yes," go to sleep this evening as you were in your youth. That point in your life when you were invincible. Order some Batman pajamas online, and wear mismatched socks to bed tonight. Before you fall asleep, think back to how it felt to be unstoppable. Not a care in the world. What did you think you were going to be when you grew up? Literally force a smile on your face as you fall asleep. Try to fall asleep in this state. When you wake up tomorrow, look at your feet and smile. Things are going to change.

Exercise #3: My Yomo's Mission Statement

A Yomo needs a core belief or value to guide its life. A Yomo needs a mission statement. Without one a Yomo will flounder aimlessly. Write a one-sentence statement to guide everything you do and every decision you make from now on. Take some time with this activity, as it is a rather lofty and challenging exercise. Use your mission statement as a guide to accomplish whatever it is that motivated you to read this book. This might be the most important step in building your Yomo.

You don't have to be an excellent writer in order to write something for yourself. Grab a pen, pencil, or even a crayon; sit down and start writing on something – paper, an old magazine, your bedroom wall. Write down the things you are consistently unhappy with in your life. Write down the things you have always wished you had. Write down the things that make you deliriously happy. Write them down, all of them, no matter how insignificant you might think they are.

As you write, start to tie the elements of what you're writing about back to yourself in a positive manner, in a way that you can proudly take ownership of them.

Research a great historical person dead or alive that you want your Yomo to emulate.

My example: King Solomon was once the King of Israel and was known to have everything a man could desire. However, he found it all meaningless and decided to pursue wisdom since he had nothing else to pursue. Solomon's labor intensive quest for knowledge, including his inquisitive nature of determining life's meaning, led him to the simplistic understanding that our time on earth is transitory and meaningless. Therefore, most of our time should be spent enjoying simplicities such as a meaningful career, a person to love, a nice dinner, a fine glass of wine (or three, in my case), and fear the Lord.

My Yomo's mission in life is to live every day in a career with passion and to help others do the same. Working in a miserable job is meaningless and futile. My Yomo strives for joy in every living day.

Although your Yomo's desires may change as life progresses, the broad generality of your Yomo's mission will remain the same. The broadness of the mission statement will help keep the Yomo in tune with larger goals.

Your mission statement should:

- Include your most important values.
- Be written in a positive context.
- Mention your biggest, most significant goals.
- Be able to serve as a day-to-day guide, as well as a long-term goal barometer.
- Start with the words "I will."

Over the next several chapters there will be activities that will refer to your mission statement. Chances are, you will need to modify or adjust your statement. That's perfectly normal. In fact, I hope your mission statement is as flexible as you are.

What is your mission statement? Write it below:

Put your mission statement somewhere you will view it every day. Allow it to be a constant reminder of everything you do.

Chapter 3: Are You Standard?

> *"And the people in the houses*
> *All went to the university,*
> *Where they were put in boxes*
> *And they came out all the same,*
> *And there's doctors and lawyers,*
> *And business executives,*
> *And they're all made out of ticky tacky*
> *And they all look just the same.*
>
> *And they all play on the golf course*
> *And drink their martinis dry,*
> *And they all have pretty children*
> *And the children go to school,*
> *And the children go to summer camp*
> *And then to the university,*
> *Where they are put in boxes*
> *And they come out all the same."*

-Malvina Reynolds

In 6th grade, my dream was to own a horse. Selling candy bars to my classmates at a 200 percent mark-up and trading my neighbors' things that I didn't think they needed. Eventually I had enough money to make my dream come true. I was a rather content 6th grader.

The only problem with owning a horse was that we lived in the city, and our backyard was the size of a bedroom. My mother came home from work one day to find me watching TV with the horse in our living room (I really should have had a babysitter until the age of 18).

Needless to say, she was horrified. I told her we needed a house with a bigger backyard.

Since I had already paid for the horse and couldn't take it back, she quickly found some land to rent and we secured the horse in an appropriate location. My mother was a real estate agent bringing me up on her own. We were not wealthy people, and she spent every extra penny she earned sending me to a private school. She didn't have the extra funds to board my horse. In fact, I think I made more money than she did at the time.

I couldn't bear to get rid of my new horse; in fact I had become rather fond of it in less than 24-hours.

Mom tried to explain to me that we could not afford a bigger house. I asked her why we couldn't just trade houses with someone else who wanted ours, and vice versa. This is how children think. She said that would only work if both owners of the homes had the same amount of equity. "What is equity?" I asked. This was the first lesson I had in finance, and I found it fascinating. She explained that we had $8,000 in equity, and our house was worth approximately $65,000.

The next day after mom went to work, I started making phone calls. I had to be careful because my mom was a real estate agent and I was calling her competitors. I couldn't let her find out what I was up to, especially since I was trying to trade our house in for a different one. Although I felt I spoke reasonably well with the real estate lingo, all the agents told me to have my parents call them back. Nobody took me seriously. I walked to the store and retrieved a free copy of "House 4-Sale by Owner."

I located a nice house for sale on one acre of land 10 miles outside of town listed at $68,000. It was perfect. Illogically, the owner of the home actually engaged my questions over the phone, which was really cool. I told him we had a house in town, and I needed a different one to appropriately board my new horse.

The owner informed me that they wanted to move into town and did not want the acreage anymore. I asked him how much equity he had in his home. He said $5,000, and would be willing to negotiate trading homes. I took his address and told him we would stop by his house in the evening.

When mom came home, I told her I had traded the house for a better one and gave her the address. She told me that my plan wouldn't work, but felt obligated to go look at the home since I already made an appointment. Forty five days later we were living on an acre, and my horse had a new home with a nice barn. We even had a huge garden, so we saved money on vegetables too. I identified where the asparagus was growing the first day we moved in and mowed it down with the lawn mower. I told mom I thought they were weeds. We now had a perfect home. One of my mom's friends told her that I was a Tasmanian Devil. In hindsight if I had known what that word meant, I would have said, "No, I'm an entrepreneur."

Being standard is nonsense, and nobody should allow himself or herself to be average. It's no secret that most of our education system is in dire need of reformation. It is a problem that is bigger than what any one of us can fix, but in my view the situation is simple: What we are spending money and time on to teach our children doesn't properly prepare them to live full and satisfying lives.

Nearly every schoolteacher is idealistic about his or her philosophy behind what education should be and what children should learn. One reason they became teachers was so they could help cultivate young minds into becoming the next great generation of thinkers and problem solvers — talents that our society will always desperately need. However, in our school systems, we reward children who are able to follow directions and provide predetermined answers to test questions.

I was definitely not rewarded for my ability to follow directions. My senior year of high school was filled with fun days in the park, skipping school, and using my fake ID to get higher paying jobs. This was easy to get away with in the 80s, but not so much today. I would apply for jobs, explaining to prospective employers I was a graduating college student with honors in finance (I was 14). Eventually I learned what the word "finance" meant and actually became pretty good at my jobs. I would read finance books at night and show up to work with new words everyday.

While I was hornswoggling my way into "important people jobs," my mom failed to inform me that people study for the SAT exams to get into college. In fact, she forgot to mention to go to college, period. Maybe she had already determined that I was going to be locked up in prison for the rest of my life.

The day after my high school graduation party, I strolled into a random classroom to take the SAT exam and fell asleep in the first portion of the test. It covered math (my nemesis), and since I had stayed up until 4 AM (not studying), a nap seemed more important. I bubbled in a cool sequence of dots before I drifted off to dream land. I read and answered the questions in the other sections, but when I received my results I decided I should have just napped through the entire thing. My test scores basically stated I was the dumbest person in the United States, and if a school were willing to take me, I would probably have to take the short bus to get to classes and would be lucky to graduate. This was quite a big difference from my last testing in the 6th grade where I ranked as a freshman in college at the age of 12. Somehow, I had regressed, but I didn't care; I didn't even know what they did in college. But then it dawned on me: You go to college to look like you're being productive, to avoid the harsh reality of determining what you are supposed to do with the rest of your life. I became determined to go to college. It sounded like YMCA camp — fun.

Later, I learned what you do in college is take more standardized tests, a lot of them. It was multiple-choice test city, and I found that my testing abilities never improved. I graduated with a 2.3 GPA. This pleased me. I passed.

In *The Element,* Sir Ken Robinson states that every person has a unique way of learning. Robinson observed schools, students, styles of learning, and creativity for years and concluded that many schools were disregarding students' unique abilities and, instead, were passing or failing them based on how well they did on a standardized test. Most schools don't have the budget or the staff to be able to teach to every student's unique learning style. The best they can do is to teach to the most economical standard. A student's ability to pass a standardized test determines whether the school receives funding. Most teachers don't want to evaluate students this way, but many do not have a choice. These standards measure empirically and show practical results of student progress to people who demand to see them.

Schools have literally been turning children, the most creative beings on earth, into the least creative people possible. Stop for a moment and consider: what did your schooling teach you?

If you managed straight A's and high marks for your entire academic career and have been successful in passing standardized tests, what do you have to show for it? Successfully passing tests and getting high scores shows future employers that you were capable of sitting in a chair while understanding and following directions, if they care at all. Most likely, if you are successful, it is because of your talents and passions rather than because of your high scores in school. Some of you may be proud to put your high school or college GPA on your resume, but how does that translate to a hiring manager? Most human resource representatives will tell you the same thing: After your first place of employment, very few people care about your grades in high school or college.

All this standardization is blinding us to the new opportunities. Imagine one evening, while eating dinner, you spill your spaghetti sauce mixed with some seasoning on a nickel, only to find after you cleaned the mess up it created the most stunningly polished nickel in the world. If your main career focus was in accounting and you worked in accounting, you would probably smile and cherish the beauty for a few moments. But, if you were following your destiny in pursuit of your highest talent and interests, you would knock over the dinner table to get to a pen and write the concoction down, have it bottled a few hours later, and start researching how you could sell it to every coin collector in the world. Unfortunately, in this situation you have been trained to be standard, and that possibility does not cross your mind.

Your primary thought is to set the alarm for 6:30 AM to meet with Frank the janitor to reduce the cost of toilet paper rolls because they don't fit in the budget anymore, and figure out how to convince employees to go to the bathroom at Burger King prior to coming to work.

Motivational speaker Anthony Robbins makes this point clear in many of his seminars globally. He asks people in his audience to count how many articles of green clothing people can see around them in the audience. Once people complete the task, he asks how many people were wearing red. Nobody knows because they were only focusing on the green. This is exactly why your spicy spaghetti sauce nickel cleaning solution will never go to market. You are an accountant; you have toilet paper issues to contend with at work.

Entrepreneurs and maverick businessmen typically don't care if their business partners or employees received good grades throughout school. They care about hiring people who are able to get the job done and bring in money. Skills like this usually can't be derived by looking at a piece of paper, which reduces everything you have done into a string of letters and numbers. They look for your assets in all your experiences, in what risks you've taken, in who you are, not what you have absorbed from a textbook. I once got a job running an IT firm because the CFO of the Phoenix Chamber of Commerce thought I was funny; they didn't care that I lacked an education in IT.

There is a lot of pressure on every student to do his or her absolute best when it comes to schooling. After all, if you do well, you are granted a certificate that says you have completed a course of education, and these are the kinds of credentials that employers look for. Not to mention people with less education have higher unemployment rates and less income. In 2010, according the Bureau of Labor Statistics (BLS), people with a high school diploma or less had a 10.3-14.9 percent unemployment rate as opposed to those with an associate's degree (7.0 percent) or a Bachelor's degree (5.4 percent). The BLS also reported that those with a high school diploma or less made $444-626 a week on average compared to those with an associates degree who make $767 a week on average or people with Bachelor's degrees who make an average of $1038 a week. All of our problems could be solved, if only we could do well in school.

Standardized tests are really good at assigning numbers to students. They aren't great at telling you what the student is like, how well they participate in class, their favorite subjects, how they best learn, what kind of life at home they have, or any of the other millions of details that make a student unique. Yet, it is the way administrators determine how well their school is doing. It is also how administrators decide whom to let into their institutions of higher education. The most mainstream offense and exploitation of the school systems is the test preparation industry.

The LSAT is a test you must pass in order to get into most law schools. It's not an easy test – seeing how it is designed to test your ability to think logically – but it is standardized, and essentially the same from year to year. Since the same test is given to every potential law student every year, TestMasters is able to design a preparation course around it by using test materials from previous year's examinations. The tests are so similar from year to year that TestMasters is able to guarantee an increase in the test-taker's score. That is assuming you have six weeks and $1,500 to take the test prep course.

To some, $1,500 is an outrageous amount of money. Most people who take the LSAT are not yet eligible for student loans to help them pay for it. Others claim that the $1,500 is just a small investment in their future and take it out on a credit card. After all, what is another $1,500 on your credit card? With today's interest rates, you could pay that off in...

The point, however, is that it doesn't matter how well you study or how well you take exams. How well you do on the LSAT seems to be largely judged on your ability to hand over $1,500. Does this say anything about your ability to practice law?

My friend Lamar Sims took the LSAT back in the early 1970s before standardized testing began. Like so many of us, Lamar wasn't certain what he wanted to do for a career after graduating with his undergraduate Liberal Arts Degree. But, after speaking to a few people, his interest in law was sparked. It was uncommon in the 70s to pay for a prep class, so Lamar just took the test blind as most people did. Back then, if you passed the LSAT it showed you most likely had the natural ability to become a lawyer. Not everyone could make it as a lawyer, that's just the way it was. He was admitted and graduated from Harvard's Law School *without paying for a prep test*. More than 30 years later, acting as Chief Deputy District Attorney for Denver, Colorado, Lamar still loves his career in law.

TestMasters has gone so far as to have their students sign an agreement stating they will not share the test materials with anyone, ever, under risk of being reported as a cheater to the BAR Association. What kind of deal is TestMasters cutting with the BAR Association to get exclusive rights to old test materials? Is making study materials available to those who can afford the documents really the best way to assess future lawyers?

It would be nice if we were all on a level playing field when competing for positions in school, but unfortunately that is a thing of the past. Isn't it ironic that standardizing tests has tilted the playing field away from those who would be good at something? We must find a way to get around standardized testing to become successful.

What Do Standardized Tests Test?

To this very day, I can't pass standardized tests, and typically rank in the 70th percentile or lower. I simply don't care about tests and don't have the patience to even read the questions. I start thinking about lunch or how good a nap would feel. At one point, I did think law school sounded entertaining and started taking practice tests for the LSAT. It took me less than 12 hours to determine that it just wouldn't work. I enjoy studying contractual law and actually do fairly well practicing as my own lawyer when battling companies over fraudulent behavior. However, I was testing in at a score so low I looked under the table to find it. No law school would ever accept me, even if I studied for the next 25 years. Yale might have considered accepting me in the psychology department though, as a testing malfunction specimen.

Standardized tests are ineffective in two ways. First, you can buy a better score by taking the prep classes, which doesn't gauge how smart you are, just how good at studying you are. And second, you can use various test taking skills and statistics to guess your way to a better grade, again eliminating any value from the test.

Henry Ford and Thomas Edison didn't have to take a standardized test. We should all be thankful for this or we probably wouldn't have a V-8 engine and we would still be using candles for lightning. Life would be one constant romantic dining experience by horse and buggy.

With a strong personal conviction that I did not enjoy math, it still didn't stop me from testing into the top five percent of all students in math when entering a master's program. These numbers were so impressive that the university offered me a greatly discounted tuition in exchange for tutoring students who were in undergraduate math courses. How did this happen? All I had to do was pick the most logical of four answers and fill in the corresponding bubble. I guessed my way into that top 5 percent. Chances are another student, one who had been working at developing their math skills for years, was probably knocked out of the running to receive a well-deserved, discounted tuition. I didn't take the position, but it was tempting.

Tests measure whether or not a person is capable of filling in a bubble. What does a standardized test not grade? Your ability to think logically and creatively.

What are two things most innovative employers look for? Logic and creativity.

This is what I have to say about standardized testing: It typically tests very little about our true abilities, and it certainly does not test talents. After testing all my life in a low percentile, I have still managed to own more than 20 companies (including one of the first online trading floors in the U.S.), follow my dreams, and believe I am successful. Furthermore, I took over the legal department of my trading floor, which is a highly litigious industry.

We were sued over 15 times, and I never lost a case when acting as the firm's council. Luckily, nothing ever went to civil court because a judge would never let me argue without a license...

The standardized tests I took told me I couldn't even win a game of hopscotch. As you can see I'm not a fan of standardized testing. Just to examine if they still are as incorrect as they have been in the past, I took a test at the age of 38 to measure my abilities and talents for a career. The test informed me I would be good in accounting. Mind you I have never balanced my checkbook, passed my accounting course above a C-, and drive my own accountants crazy because I categorize everything under "miscellaneous." The only part of my personality that would be suited for an accounting position is the fact that I can write checks.

Standardized testing creates standardized thinkers and learners. This results in a very narrow selection of job candidates for employers to pick from. Taking a career based on a standard education results in a particular kind of job – cubicle walls, fluorescent lighting, coworkers who can only create conversation based on something they watched on television the night before. It is now more important than ever to find ways to make yourself unique to employers. Diversify yourself.

Exercise #4: Superhero Sized Strengths

Let's give your Yomo some strengths. Add strengths to your Yomo that you would like yourself. If you are coming up short, ask your friends, coworkers, and/or bosses. Consider buying the book *Strength Finder 2.0*. This is the best test I have seen on the market, and was compiled from 30 years of personality research. Everyone should take this test, but you have to buy the book to get the code. It's a fine marketing tactic I must say. The test lists your innate strengths, suggests professions, and guides you on how to strengthen your strengths. It told me that I should be a motivational speaker and/or an educator. You have lots of strengths, go find them.

My strengths and some strengths that my Yomo has include:
Visionary
Very charismatic
Enjoys people
Sarcastic
Rarely serious

Write a combination of strengths you now possess and those you would like to have below. Then take time each day to focus on these strengths.

Exercise #5: My Exceptional Skills

Your Yomo does certain things at an exceptional level over other Yomos. What are these things?

Now is not the time to be modest. What is that one ace up your sleeve that you pull out at parties or at dinner with friends that can't be topped? How did you acquire that skill?

What do you wish you could do better than anyone else? How does your mission statement reflect that?

My example:
I am excellent at motivating people to become their best
I inspire people to achieve
I enjoy life and make people laugh
I love to link new ideas together
I love to try the unknown

Write the skills you excel at below. Also write the skills you want to possess. Take time each day to think about how awesome you are.

Chapter 4: Changing Our Mind Games

"You don't have a soul. You are a soul; you have a body."
-C.S. Lewis

Brains are absolutely incredible machines. In addition to handling the day-to-day activities you don't even think about: breathing, walking, blinking your eyes, digesting your food, etc.; they also filter through billions of bits of information which surround us all day every day. Brains create memories, process information, and take old information and tie it together to create new ideas. Our brains are not only our personalized tools for survival; they are also the driving force of our civilization's progress.

However, the brain is unlike any machine we humans have ever been able to engineer. Unlike most machines, which are designed to do very specific things, our brains can be transformed to do or create whatever we need it to. Not only do they help us perform tasks, but our brains can also create opportunities and realities just through the function of neurons and neural networks. If we want something to become a truth and reality, then through the power of using our brains to think about it, we make it happen. Acquiring the career you have always dreamed about depends on one thing: your ability to make your thoughts affect your brain in the method you desire. Literally, to get your dream job you just need to think about it.

The Yomo, which you are working towards building in the final exercise, will serve as a constant beacon – a reminder – of the career you ultimately aspire to have.

It is a symbol upon which you will focus your thoughts to change your brain patterns. Through the Yomo, I will demonstrate how you can think your way into the perfect career. After all, your reality is what you think about constantly. Feed your brain the thoughts of the reality you desire, and you will be working the career you want, eventually. It is very important to understand that your brain does not know what reality is. Whatever thought you decide to give your brain then becomes the reality your brain comprehends. If you tell your brain that you can't do something enough times, your brain will make it true. Your thoughts are what make things happen, not your brain.

Our mind reflects what it is fed every day. You need a better diet. You mind creates reality. Our brains reinforce network connections through repetition. These connections become stronger and more difficult to break.

This chapter is largely about the brain and how it works. It is the largest chapter of the book so do not stray. To properly explain how to best use your brain I will need to use some scientific terms. Fret not. I know I am not alone when I say that it takes me a long time to wrap my mind around ideas that are not tangible. This is why I will be using a lot images and analogies to explain these ideas.

To start thinking about how the brain works, let us first consider something more tangible that we can all relate to, a car. The work you put into a car is like the work we should be putting into our brains. At first a car just needs an annual tune-up, perhaps a wax and shine. Once in a while it will need a new tire. As it gets older it requires a bit more work, replacing hoses and belts, repairing upholstery, fixing dents, stopping windshield cracks. A car that has been on the road for 15 years can easily be driven for another 15 years if it is maintained properly and the owner is conscious of what the car needs. If the owner is willing to invest the time and care into a car as it ages, the value can be maintained and even increased (think of a cherry '65 Mustang).

Your brain is much the same way. Like cars, if we neglect our brains they will eventually cease working. Keeping both our brains and our cars in optimal condition requires a bit of attention, knowhow, and regular maintenance. After we have driven the same car for a few years, we understand what noises it usually makes and we have a feel for how it operates. At the same time, we know when something is wrong with it when it sounds or feels different. The same attention is required of our brains – we have to know what to watch for when our brain isn't being as efficient or powerful as it could be.

Like driving, our brain operation can easily go into autopilot. If you have been driving a car for a few years, you have probably fallen into some driving habits. You know what you need to do to safely start and operate the car. Beyond that, many of us fall into autopilot, subconsciously knowing what we need to do to get from point A to point B – the mindless commute to our office or the grocery store. We know that we have to move our foot to the left to stop without thinking, "Press the left pedal to stop." Though you do this automatically when you drive, I bet you had to visually think for a few seconds and run the process in your mind to see if that last sentence was correct. That is autopilot.

It is very easy for our brains to fall into the same habit-based operations. Thanks to our tech-savvy culture, we are always finding ways to put things in autopilot in the name of "making life simpler." In fact, as we'll later learn, if it weren't for our frontal lobes we wouldn't be able to learn how to do anything new or develop new thinking; we would be on permanent autopilot. We would do the exact same tasks day in and day out in order to meet our needs.

In order to become better thinkers and innovators, and in order to embark on a career path we enjoy, we need to become conscious of our mental processes. Just as we tune up our automobiles to make them run better, we can change the way we think to be more productive and innovative. Time to take out your tools and roll up your sleeves.

Your Neural Networks

Note for the science part: Read this as many times as you need to fully engage the concepts.

Ever have one of those days where your mind is all over the place and you can't seem to focus on one thing long enough to get it done? It's as if your brain is scrambled and an absolute mess. Guess what, all things considered, your brain is a mess.

If you were to look at a brain through a microscope, you would see a jumble of string-like neural networks, attached, disjointed, unattached, starting in one place and seemingly ending in the middle of nowhere. Your brain looks like a tangled box of Christmas lights after they have spent the past year in the attic. It's a spectacular mess.

Instead of Christmas lights, however, these neural networks make up everything about your thinking and your personality. They are made up of billions of neurons, which come together throughout your life.

Neurons travel to and from our brains through nerve paths to process information, think of new ideas, and react to outside stimuli. Most of these neural networks cross, overlap, and intersect millions of times. Our brains represent the exact definition of a network: A system of circuits with lots of connections and intersections. For example, if I were to ask you to visualize shaking the callused hand of an 80-year-old man who has been gardening all his life and holds a twinkle in his eye because he has loved his career for the last 30 years, could you picture this? I bet you just did. Even though you may have never engaged in this opportunity, you pulled from different neural networks to create the picture. You have probably seen an 80-year-old man, know what someone looks like when they are happy, felt a callused hand in the past (probably your own), and have seen a twinkle in someone's eye in the past. In essence, you pulled from old neural networks and created a new picture in your head that you have never seen before, but the picture was probably very clear. You just created a new neural pathway that did not exist 10 seconds ago.

When your brain creates a new neural pathway it does it in the most economical way it can. The ends of two neurons relay information through a tiny gap (called the synaptic gap), with neurotransmitters. Your brain doesn't waste the material needed to close the gap to transfer the information, but instead sends out neurotransmitters to carry the message for it.

After a while the brain knows what neural pathways to use to accomplish a desired result. The brain will then tune itself to a certain frequency to push messages along a preferred neural pathway. As these networks are used more frequently, they will become stronger and help develop your preferred mindset.

Through decades of research, doctors and scientists have identified the functions that each section, or lobe, of the brain performs. It wasn't until the most recent evolution of humans that we started to see an increase in the size of our frontal lobes, which control our higher reasoning and thinking.

The frontal lobe is the very part of our brains that allows humans to be superior to just about every other species. But what does it do? And why should someone looking to have a fantastic career care about it?

Think for a moment about the typical day of a dog: Boston (my old lab), wakes up, eats the carpeting, stretches out, looks at the food bowl to be fed, and scratches at the door to be let outside (if I was lucky). Then he spends the day either sleeping or chewing a hole in my favorite pair of shoes. Some days you may think Boston is the dumbest creature on earth. While he may not seem bright, he still has a frontal lobe, which he uses to learn how to acquire food, what he needs to do to get attention and other pleasurable stimuli, and to be trained where it is proper to relieve himself.

We humans, however, require a little more brainpower in our day-to-day activities. Our senses are tuned to accept billions of bits of information a day. It is up to our frontal lobe to filter out most of the stimuli our senses collect and decide what is important and worth paying attention to. The frontal lobe is also an important player when it comes to learning new things. When new information comes along that we want to remember, our frontal lobe creates new neural networks to keep us from forgetting the valuable information. After the neural pathway has been solidified, the frontal lobe pushes it out into the rest of our brain for storage and then resumes work on filtering and creating new neural networks.

Imagine that neural networks are like Aspen trees. When you have a thought it is planted like a seed. The more you think about the thought, it grows into a tree with branches (related thoughts) and a strong trunk. When we are not thinking about the network it gets filed in the "back" of our brains, but stays connected through the "roots" like Aspen trees. If you are unfamiliar with Aspen trees, one grove is actually one organism connected through the roots. Pretty in the mountains, pain in the rear end when you plant one in your yard and it sprouts into your foundation. Anyway, when we add more neural networks to our brain and connect seemingly unrelated thoughts, we create a forest of connected tree-like networks. Those connections are innovative thinking, experimenting "outside the box."

The frontal lobe connects neural networks billions of times a day and all through the night. The information that we acquire during the day is continually being processed, even in our sleep. While we are unconscious, our brain is looking for new neural networks it can connect the fresh information with. Often this comes across to us in the form of a dream; some scientists even go as far as to say our mind runs out to the quantum field to retrieve more information. This may explain why your last dream involved flying around in diapers with boa feathers wrapped around your head. Our brain works purely off of stimuli it receives — it is incapable of producing totally new thoughts on its own. Each idea we have is simply the culmination of information and thoughts we have already acquired.

Sometimes the frontal lobe assists in deciding what is worth noticing. It can take information you come across and help tie it with a neural network to an existing memory to become more permanent. This is why a smell might remind you of a seemingly unimportant childhood memory. Since your frontal lobe acts as a filter to all of the stimuli you come across each day, it is important that we take our brains off of autopilot and learn how to take control of that filter. You must consciously decide what is worth noticing and paying attention to. This starts with being more observant of your surroundings. It ends with consciously deciding what information and stimuli matters.

For example, say you needed to remember a set of driving directions (for the sake of this example, let's assume you left your cell phone and your GPS at home). When someone gives you the directions, you can either write them down or repeat them to yourself in your head. Both of these actions initiate the building of a new neural network in your brain.

When you write down the directions you light up the neural network once, and you probably won't light it up again until you next think about those directions. By repeating those directions, or even just thinking about them, you are strengthening that neural network. All of the neurons are connected, and neurotransmitters are sending signals along the network, all of them looking to expand the network to other relevant information. For example, how long a mile is, what various landmarks are in that area, the proper procedure for making a left turn, or maybe it is trying to outline your journey on the map of the city you have built inside your head. The more you repeat the same information, the stronger the pathways inside your head become.

Dreams are theorized to be the brain finding new connections for information we gathered during the day. That's why we connect images like diapers and boa feathers. Think of the frontal lobe as having a finite amount of RAM. At night it purges the RAM — packed away in long-term memory. Your best thoughts come in the morning, because you have maximum RAM available.

"Each idea we have is simply the culmination of information and thoughts we have already acquired." Creativity is associating this information in new ways.

The mind is simply an operating system the brain created to allow the human to focus. There is so much stimulus coming to the brain all day, by focusing attention we are able to better predict future outcomes. We are prediction machines. Often, stress is created when we can't predict (with some certainty), the future. The reality we perceive is not reality. This point is proven over and over again. It's the reality our mind creates. Think of it as an operating system or model that the brain created.

At the age of 13, I started requesting stock for Christmas. When I became a full grown adult at the age of 14, I knew what a ticker symbol was (all my friends were clueless about this language; hence me being an adult) and began investing in business suits. Successful people wore them, and I was certain I would need one soon. I then proceeded to sell everything in my father's house that wasn't bolted down in order to practice the art of negotiation, while wearing my suits of course. I was unaware at the time that I could have just read a book on the subject matter.

After finishing my masters degree in my mid twenties, I cashed in the stock I had been accumulating over the years, pulled out my suits, found some partners, and opened one of the first online trading firms in the world. I had this vision at the age of 14, and I accomplished the task down to what the desk looked like in my office from my vision. I didn't necessarily visualize a trading floor as a teenager because I didn't know what one was at the time; but I did visualize the sense of power of running a company down to wearing those crazy suits. By the age of 30, I had more than 20 subsidiary companies launched, forging the way to some of the most incredible technological advancements history had seen at the time. We were making millions on the trading floor, and I owned everything I could possibly desire. This time my suits had Armani tags rather than K-Mart embroidery. The neural networks I built when I was 14 years of age allowed me to focus on my vision over the long term and led to the fulfillment of my dreams in my 20s. I created a fictitious neural pathway in my head that later became my reality.

Is this starting to make a little sense?

The process of building neural networks happens billions of times a day when you have information to learn, recall, or develop. When you recognize a friend on the street, a new pathway lights up that connects to other stored neural networks reminding you of details about that person. Seeing their face sends information flying around to different parts of that network to bring up their name, or why they might be in this end of town at this time, or details and questions they brought up in your last conversation, maybe the names of their family members so you can ask about their well being. All of this happens in nanoseconds.

When you apply for a new job with a company, you are probably going to emphasize the skills you have been working on for years. The employer knows, subconsciously, that the more you already know how to do, the less they'll have to teach you. This will result in less time to develop strong neural pathways (sometimes called "the learning curve"), which will make you a more productive employee sooner. Assuming, of course, the job fits with the kind of employee you want to be. Telling an employer you have already visualized the process probably won't help you get the job, but it will change your life later.

Physics: Take the Quantum Leap

Believe it or not, quantum physics doesn't have to be scary. As appalled as I am with the extensive language applied to the field of neurobiology, I find the lingo used in any type of physics to be even more troubling. Over the last 100 years the word "quantum" has continuously been one of those words that seemed to exist purely in the realm of science fiction and theoretical physics. However, as we are able to harness more energy and produce greater results in the scientific world, quantum physics becomes more real and tangible.

That being said, quantum physics is still a very complicated and uncertain science. I can only explain so much in these pages because I am not a quantum mechanics specialist, I just pretend to be one. Why then did I bring up quantum physics? Because there is one very specific principle of quantum physics that is central to helping you create the life and career you most want: Your consciousness affects subatomic particles.

Let me help you with the Wiki definition so you don't have to put this book down and run to your computer:

> In particle physics, the conceptual idea of a particle is one of several concepts inherited from classical physics. This describes the world we experience, for example, to describe how matter and energy behave at the molecular scales of quantum mechanics. <u>For physicists, the word "particle" means something rather different from the common sense of the term, reflecting the modern understanding of how particles behave at the quantum scale in ways that differ radically from what everyday experience would lead us to expect.</u>

I have underlined the critical portion of the definition.

This principle basically states that you are able to affect outcomes just by thinking about them. When it gets boiled down, the principle seems rather obvious: our brains are conductors of energy, and atoms are affected by this energy. Think about how magnets or wind works; they have a force capable of affecting metals, an invisible energy that relocates entire houses if the gust or magnetic force is strong enough.

The particle or neuron is less important than the network it's connected to. We are finding that the neuron can be part of multiple networks in the brain simultaneously — as if it's in a quantum state.

Few know it, and even fewer may admit it, but many religions have been subscribing to the principle ideas of quantum physics for centuries. The power of prayer — repetitive, focused thinking on a certain topic — can very well result in a desirable outcome. The development of your Yomo is very similar to that. By taking the time to consciously think about the outcome and by setting up visual and physical reminders of that desired outcome, the dream will become reality.

Henry Ford may not have invented the automobile, but he invented a whole new way of producing them. By perfecting the assembly line method of car manufacturing, he was able to sell thousands of cars a month, give jobs to people who weren't necessarily mechanically inclined, and invent a totally new lifestyle for the American people.

Henry Ford is also famous for patenting the V-8 engine. He had watched his engineers put together 32-valve, 4-cylinder, and 6-cylinder engines. So why not put together an 8-cylinder engine?

Ford approached his engineers with this idea. They initially told him it was impossible. For the better part of two years, they told him they couldn't figure out a way to do it. Until one day, the engineers figured it out.

Ford had the image in his head of what he wanted, and he didn't stop thinking about it until he got it.

Let's get back to religion. Assuming you believe that objective truth does exist and can be known, does that mean Christians, Muslims, pagans, atheists, and Jews can all be right in their respective beliefs in God? No. If this were true it would break the law of non-contradiction. Only one religion can be correct or else the theory contradicts itself. This is one of the reasons so many people are confused about religion: it takes time and research to determine the truth, and it is easier to create our own terms of understanding. Look at how powerful our thoughts are — we have religious wars over this stuff. People would rather kill each other than educate themselves to see who is right and who is wrong. The power of thought is mind boggling because all these sects have created their own reality, and within each reality, they are right. If people can convince themselves that they were created by a man wearing a dress flying around on a horse with wings, could you potentially create a reality as to what your career will look like? Of course you can! No killing need be involved. Great majorities of people don't know why they believe in what they believe. They just know other people are wrong. Can you explain why you are right in your spiritual beliefs? Did you create a reality based from fiction? Non-fiction? Do you even know?

Rewiring your neural pathways to develop a positive thought process will do wonders when it comes to acquiring the career you want. If you are consciously moving ions around in a positive mindset, the ions will spread to other parts of your body. Various hormones and good-feeling chemicals will flood your system. Your outlook will become significantly more positive, and you will become much more proactive when it comes to achieving your goals.

The backbone of therapy is the idea of replacing cues (things that trigger a negative or unwanted behavior), with a different behavior. For example, think of a fond childhood memory, eat a chocolate chip cookie. Get fat. Once you identify your trigger, you replace the cue with a different behavior like call mom. This strengthens your relationship rather than making you fat. The only issue at that point is to reinforce that network connection in your brain so it becomes as strong as the old connection. NOTE: you won't eliminate the old connection. It's there. So you need to make the new one as strong or stronger.

No line of thought, or ability, or skill set is out of reach. Just as no one who first picks up a guitar has any idea what they are doing. But after years of focused practice, even the least musically minded person can become an accomplished musician, assuming they enjoy doing it.

While our brains may be a powerful mess of neurons, it is possible to develop and define certain neural networks to our benefit. A neurological study was conducted at Harvard in the mid-90s with university students to see exactly how repetition affects memory and ability. The students in the study were asked to work with the scientists and a piano to monitor how plastic the brain could potentially be.

The first group of subjects were taught to play a five note sequence, which they were asked to play on the piano for two hours a day for five days. The second group was given the piano and no instruction at all, but was still asked to play for two hours a day for the five days. The third group was asked to observe the first group as they played and learn, visually, how the notes were played.

The fourth group, the control group in this experiment, was asked to do nothing with a piano. They didn't even need to show up.

The results of this experiment were very enlightening regarding the effects of controlled thoughts. Using a collection of expensive technological equipment, the scientists were able to monitor changes in the subjects' neural networks. They noticed that the changes in the subjects from group three (the subjects who watched the piano players) were consistent with the changes in group one (the piano players playing the sequence). The second group (the group that was not given the sequence) had limited neural changes. However, the changes were not as significant as groups one and three. Those in the control group experienced no neural changes at all. The common thread? Mental repetition. The first and third groups were able to play and observe the same note sequence over and over, while the second group had no focus in regards to what notes they were playing.

In other words, participants grew neural networks simply by watching other people and thinking about the task.

In another study, subjects were asked to test the strength of their fingers with rubber bands. The control group was asked to exercise their fingers with a rubber band for 30 minutes a day. The second group was asked to think about exercising their fingers for 30 minutes a day. The result? The control group responded with a 28 percent increase in strength in their fingers. The second group? Twenty two percent. Impressive.

The second group didn't even do anything but think (try not to use this as an excuse to never work out again). This presents an excellent case for the power of thought in developing reality. How then can you apply this information to getting the career you want?

The Science of Personality

Over the years there have been thousands of motivational speakers who all have a very similar idea: You have the power to change your life to be anything you want it to be. Most of their messages are the same, and their techniques come from every school of thought, but the underlying method is the same — repetition. If you are able to remember a simple phone number or set of directions through the very basic principle of repeating it in your head until it sticks, just think of what you'll be able to do if you repeat other ideas.

The science is simple: Repetition creates strong connections, and strong connections equate to strong abilities.

The same goes for the personality you develop. Your thoughts become moods. Your moods affect and develop your habits. After several years, these habits develop into your personality. Even the most basic thought will create a personality if you focus on it long enough. For example, you have a neighbor who has a loud yappy dog. The dog is really annoying, and so you think, "I hate that dog." Every day you see or hear the little dog you think, "I hate that dog." Pretty soon whenever you see any little dog, or hear any yappy bark, and you think, "I hate that dog." Eventually you become a person who hates dogs, just from one little thought, you repeated over and over.

In chapter two, I had you go sleep in mismatched socks thinking childlike thoughts. Did you do it? If you did, you created a neural network. If you go to bed with those childlike thoughts repeatedly, that network will eventually become strong enough to become a mental habit, and you will truly be able to do anything, just as you believed when you were a child.

The neural connections we create determine everything about our personality. Strong neural connections are the things we know how to do easily, and those connections are what employers look for when hiring (that "quick learner" trait). On the same note, the type of personality traits we have work on a similar level. Whether someone is inherently positive or pessimistic or lazy or a workaholic depends on what set of personality-based neurons they have been working on for their entire life. Someone who is lazy and avoids work probably learned at a young age that not working equates to pleasure. So he or she kept doing it, and the neuron connection grew stronger until the idea of doing any work at all became revolting to him or her. The same goes for those who are hard workers, or optimists, or negative-nancies.

The wonderful thing about the brain and the frontal lobe is that you can change it to do your bidding. Again, your thoughts are the one tool you have to change your brain to do what you want it to do. Once you know how it is wired, you can begin to rewire it. The same way the frequent use of a neural network creates a stronger connection, not using it can atrophy the connection. You can rewire your brain to think your way to the Yomo you are designing.

My ultimate goal is to help you create your Yomo to be exactly who you want to be. The Yomo will then serve as a guide, a plan, for you to shape your mental thinking through. It will be a constant reminder of what you are working towards so you will be able to know which direction to go next. In other words, we will be building a new neural network and calling it your Yomo.

Developing a Learning Process

According to the Motorola University, students typically retain five percent of what they hear, 10 percent of what they read, 20 percent of what they read and hear at the same time, and 30 percent of what they have had demonstrated to them. These types of instruction equate to what is known as "passive learning." However, if a teacher is able to facilitate "participatory learning," the information retention makes significant leaps. If a student participates in a discussion group, they retain 50 percent, if they take a hands-on approach, 75 percent. If a student is then asked to teach a particular subject to others, he or she retains 90 percent of the information.

This concept is based on the idea that the more senses

you engage when acquiring new information, the more likely you are to remember it. As I discussed in the last chapter, every single person learns a little differently. However, the one constant for all of us when it comes to learning is this: the more senses that are engaged in the learning process, the stronger the related neural network will be. Just like how the more muscle groups you have engaged while exercising will create a stronger body.

The same is true when developing your Yomo. Throughout the book, I am having you revisit your Yomo in a way that asks you to think about and engage with it a little bit differently each time. I am also asking you to think about your Yomo in a very tangible, participatory way. Doing so will create a neural network, changing the way you think to make your ideal become a reality.

Open your eyes. Break from the routine. Read the section of the paper you always ignore, wander the part of the bookstore you have never bought from. Take a walk through your neighborhood, try a new food, have a conversation with a stranger. Engage the frontal lobe and develop new neural networks. A curious, innovative mind is within your grasp. Once you have a strong set of neural networks that are geared towards fulfilling your Yomo, then you will see the opportunities for your dream career.

Look! A Squirrel!

Focusing on one thing can be the hardest part of changing a new career. Creating new neural networks that work needs repetition and *focus*. Some of us have attention spans of squirrels, others let our fears divert us back to our old paths, and still others just simply lack staying power. This is a skill we need to develop. We must build neural networks and focus on specifics; otherwise the chance of your success is in danger.

My focus, or lack thereof, has always been a problem. Most people can't think of one thing they would love to do. I, on the other hand, can think of a new thing I want to try on a daily, if not hourly, basis. It took years of failure before I understood that once I start something, I needed to follow through and finish. I literally have to try hard not to have thoughts outside of what I am building in the moment. The most exhausting portion of my life is trying NOT to think of cool things to create or accomplish. I do have the attitude that I can accomplish anything because it is my reality. Whatever bubble I put myself in remains real. The trick is to avoid creating too many realities at once.

After I built my online stock-trading floor, I became bored with all my riches and success. I also happened to notice that all my friends who had children complained about how fast their offspring grew and how expensive it was to keep them clothed. After a day of trading, making thousands of dollars, I pondered how to make an enormous exchange system of used children's clothing at a low cost. Just like the Auto Trader for cars, only trading kid's jumper suits and tiny shoes. I lost interest in this quickly because I didn't have children, and I didn't know how to talk to the people who owned them. They weren't really profit-and-loss type of folks and my spreadsheets scared them.

Making far too much money, my innovative mind on idle, I started looking at different angles to challenge myself, while money literally just poured into my couch seats. Porn, in the late 1990s, was one of the most profitable businesses on the Internet, which intrigued me. I wasn't into porn, but I had to research the arena to see how I could take a slightly different angle and capitalize on the market. I would just use an alias so my family and friends wouldn't refer to me as "Miss Melissa, the Porn Queen." My grandmother would have for sure disowned me if that leaked out.

I hired someone to build and manage the site, because I would have nothing to do with porn. In hindsight, this shows a bit of insanity, since I was still willing to profit from it. I convinced one of my broke friends to join me in the endeavor in an attempt to assist her with her financial issues. As I began a full day of online research (with disgust) in the Pink Pussycat, my IT manager from the trading firm I owned decided to provide me a detailed description of how servers work on the trading floor. Seemed odd, but I stopped to listen.

After an hour of elaboration, I asked him what the point was, and I informed him that I could not care less how servers operate. That's why I paid him $75,000 per year to run the stupid things. In summary, I guess he could see all the sites I was visiting on the main server, and he was wondering, his face in a distinctly red hue and sweating profusely, if I needed to be admitted into a sexual addiction clinic.

Thoughts of my Catholic grandmother came to mind, and I quickly dumped the idea, losing 5k to my porn site developer. I decided to hire my broke friend to work in the accounting department instead of running a porn site. I temporarily lost my morals on that idea, and I needed to get back to a more respectful career that was true to who I am, and stop obsessing about being the biggest and best. Plus, I felt I did my friend a great disservice, so I needed to give her a job so she could buy more wine to recover from my terrible idea.

God (or whoever you think is at play for our existence), does funny things to people. He assisted in my boredom, lack of focus, and unethical behavior by taking everything away from me. The market crashed in 2001, and in less than 90 days I lost everything due to the economy and a lot of other dumb things. Finding myself in corporate bankruptcy court a year later, the only thing I had to ponder was the color of my rental car because I had to sell my Porsche, BMW, and my big, loud, black Dodge Ram. The days of the Porsche and the BMW were lost in a haze. I learned the Geo Metro was faster than the Ford Escort going uphill. I still had my Armani suits though, and I would wear them with great pride in my green Yugo. Then I had a thought. Perhaps I would call the Yugoslavian manufacturer and tell them how to make a real vehicle, and they might split the profits with me if I could get it to go 140 mph. I just needed to figure out how to make a new turbo charged engine fit into a really crappy car for $100. Hmmm, my uncle was a mechanical engineer. I left a message for him to start work on the blue prints, but for some reason he never called me back.

Serial entrepreneurs find enormous difficulties remaining focused. This tends to be a negative that works against the building of a strong neural network. As I stated before, repetition is critical. If you have constant new thoughts that you can't hone in on, the neural network will never have time to build around them. Much like the piano players who were never given the notes and were asked to play on their own.

If your talents are the same as mine and your specialization is creativity, then spending too much time on one endeavor will eventually bore you. However, you must stay focused on one project long enough for it to come to fruition. I have seen a lot of really dumb ideas work, including selling "pet rocks" for millions (the same rocks as the free ones we find on the side of the road). Your idea has a great chance of making it big if you stay focused. Don't stop because something costs too much to develop. Let your neural network develop it for you. If the idea is good, and you have thought long and hard about it, someone will pay for your thoughts. Persistence and focus are critical.

Exercise #6: Traits to Trash

We want to have an indicator of what your Yomo is clearly NOT. We never want to focus on our weaknesses, but want others to know what our Yomo does not like to do. This way you can surround your Yomo with other Yomos who like to do this stuff for you.

My Yomo hates to:
Sit in an office
Do anything detailed
Manage people
Run things at a micro level
Follow a long string of instructions
Shop
Do the same thing over and over again
Talk to negative people

Write your list of will-nots below and on the next page. Envision taking these attributes and throwing them in the garbage can. Your Yomo will never do these things.

Exercise #7: Work My Yomo Likes

Not all jobs are terrible. But the goal is to have a job that fully rocks, so let's list the parts of work you like the best. Detail the components of a career your Yomo will accept from potential employers. This could be multiple things, but not title-specific. Try not to title jobs as you would see in listings on Monster.com or university degrees. So no CFO, accountant, public relations agent, human resource person.

My example:
Entertain
Motivate
Speak to large audiences
Build projects at a macro level
Travel the globe to educate on anything
Inspire people

Write the part of jobs you like below and focus on them everyday along with your strengths, skills and mission statement.

Chapter 5: Innovation Shapes Our World

"When all think alike, then no one is thinking."
                                                    -Walter Lippmann

"Capital isn't so important in business. Experience isn't so important. You can get both these things. What is important is ideas. If you have ideas, you have the main asset you need, and there isn't any limit to what you can do with your business and your life."
                                                    -Harvey Firestone

"Great is the human who has not lost his childlike heart."
                                        -Mencius (Meng-Tse), 4th century BCE

An old business colleague of mine is a well-established agent within the IRS. One of his many job responsibilities is to teach organizations the workings of the tax law and Federal code (yawn). But, if you were to walk into his office you might think he was a little – odd. Dozens of hand puppets hang on his walls, which he uses to teach classes on auditing. He claims that we learn best when we learn as children. By using the puppets, he is tapping into our child-like mindset to more effectively teach the required information.

And it works. He even kept my attention.

Another one of my old colleagues and closest friends, Debbie Sprague, has worked at the IRS for nearly 30 years. Her specialization is customer service. People love her. She forgets to wear her shoes to work in the Federal Building, and people don't care. She hates wearing shoes. If you notice she is not wearing shoes, she will ask why you are so inconsiderate as to not notice how pretty her dress is. She will smile with a twinkle in her eye as you consider her question. Why spend time staring at someone's feet? Debbie is so innovative in the way that she deals with people that she gets thank you letters from companies for collecting debts from them. How weird is that?

An innovative mindset is just one of the many tools you'll need to embark on a new and challenging career, but I have to say it is one of the most important. What does it mean to be innovative? Innovation means you have the ability and the courage to put together a new way of doing things with the old methods, tools, and products. You are inventing something completely new out of what has already been used. Being innovative in the professional world means having the ability to solve problems and create solutions unlike any that have ever been seen. Innovative companies, the companies that are creating products and methods that are changing the world, don't want solutions that just anyone can come up with; they want solutions that they can call their own. Solutions they can patent and make a fortune off of, solutions that they can claim as their own.

Google is famous for the design of its offices. More than anything, they look like playgrounds. Some rooms look better suited to babysit children, with bean bag chairs and flat screen TVs, ping pong tables and slides, than to create and design code for the products they are so well known for. Could the fact that Google allows their employees to think and act like children be reason for its enormous success? Allowing its employees to let their imaginations run wild has allowed Google to take the online experience and the ability to search for information to a place that was unfathomable merely a decade ago.

However, every day on Google campuses around the

world failure happens. Designers and coders run around with ideas. They aren't good ideas or bad ideas; they are just completely new ideas. In 2010, Google announced they had invented a car that could drive itself in a city. Moreover, the car had already been driving itself all over California. Can you imagine the development meeting where a project manager walked in and said, "I want to create a car that can drive itself." Only an innovative company with innovative personnel (perhaps with a cocked eyebrow), would say, "Sure, go for it."

That engineer had to think differently in order to make the project a success. He had to look at the way we have been driving for the past century and determine what needs to happen to safely take control from the driver. Sensors, robotics and software had to be rewritten, redesigned, invented, and installed on the car to create a contraption in real life that had been originally invented for cartoons and science fiction.

You have to wonder if product developers at General Motors are kicking themselves for not thinking of it first.

Google harbors a truly innovative society in their offices and, as a result, they are going to single-handedly go down in history as coming up with some of the biggest changes in mainstream culture. We have to ask: Why isn't every company doing this? Why isn't every employee striving to come up with ideas that would take their company to a whole new level?

Developing Your Personal Innovative Style

There is no step-by-step guide to developing your own style of innovation. Anyone who claims they have written it is a liar. Innovation is built from within, from years of hard work, and from not being afraid to try new things.

If you try it, I think you may find it feels good.

The best piece of advice I can give you when it comes to developing your own personal innovative style is to start at the end. Innovation is a curious process. As a result, you need to be curious about things you have never thought about before. Your neural networks need all the stimulation they can get in order to become stronger and more interconnected. It is the only way you will be able to make connections no one else has ever come up with before. Neural networks that make unprecedented connections are what eventually become innovative ideas.

One way to keep curious is to never stop playing. Play around with ideas related to what you love to do. Is there a better way to do it? Is there a better product to be invented? Everything has fundamentals; start experimenting with them. What if you did everything backwards? Even if your hypothesis is wrong, isn't it good to know why things work a certain way? More support for your neural networks.

It is just as important to develop a personal style of innovative thinking, as it focuses your thinking on what you're great at (which we'll get to in the next chapter). Just as your personality gives you an edge in interviews, a personal innovative thinking style will give you an edge over other people in competition for the jobs at your dream company. If you start your own business, the way you do things may be the one thing that gives you an edge over the other businesses you're competing with.

People who make their living as entrepreneurs or business owners have done so because they didn't allow anyone to tell them how to think, how to do things, or that their ideas were too crazy to be successful. Chances are, if they are going to hire you to join their team, they want someone who is able to think innovatively.

Henry Ford. Bill Gates. Mark Zuckerberg. Three leaders in their fields who revolutionized the auto, computer, and social networking industries because they didn't let anyone tell them they were wrong. Their ideas may have been crazy and unmanageable, but never standard. Ford's employees considered him crazy when he asked for a V-8 engine, until they succeeded in engineering his dream.

Ford is just one of the many names brought up in classrooms when teachers tell their students that they can be anything when they grow up. Your goal in developing the Yomo is to get back to the point when anything was possible. I want everyone to live in a world where their minds are constantly stimulated and cultivated and not afraid to take risks on new ideas.

How to Find an Innovative Job

There is no great way to sugarcoat it: most job hunting sites out there today are absolute garbage. I'm sure most companies who start up a website don't aim for it to be garbage, but many sites have evolved into job hunting sites that make finding a great job next to impossible, especially if you are interested in an exceptional career. A lot of career sites are interested in one thing: Making money.

Their for-profit models are similar to the ones universities use: the more people they can claim they match with a job, the more users they will ultimately collect. However, unlike universities, job sites could not care less if you are matched up to the right job. Their primary concern is gaining traffic and selling advertising. Have you ever noticed how much spam you get when registering on a career site?

Companies who can afford to list on sites like Monster.com are after the best talent out there. They don't care if the best talent is actually right for the position advertised. It shouldn't be any surprise when you discover that the listings aren't entirely accurate and they use some pretty fluffy language to describe their available positions. More times than not, the actual job or company described is nothing like the real job in and of itself.

National corporations have also taken to using the Internet as a tool to weed out potential applicants before they even have a chance to meet them. Have you ever been asked by a company to take a personality test online when you send in your resume? These are not personality tests to determine who you are. Using a series of multiple-choice questions they determine whether or not you would be a good manager or sales representative. Before they even read your resume, they boil you down to a few letters and numbers, just like in school. Would you really want to work for people who choose their employees that way? Are these "personality" tests even accurate? The last one I took said I should be an accountant. I have never balanced my checkbook and never intend to do so in the future. Most tests should be taken for fun... Don't base your life around them.

Craigslist has become the anything goes version of a job

hunting site. Employers who post the ads aren't screened like Monster or Career Builder. The job posting may be a few lines that vaguely describe the job and instructions on how to apply. After you've spent valuable time refining your resume to match the job description you send it to a totally anonymous address with thousands of other eager candidates.

The hiring representative is then inundated with thousands of resumes and cover letters, in addition to the mountains of spam that frequently goes through Craigslist. Most representatives take the first five candidates they receive and run them through the interview process. The whole ordeal is arbitrary and informal. You may feel more appreciated applying for a job at McDonalds, though they probably use Craigslist as well.

The current mainstream method for recruiting new employees does not work. Online job search engines aim to make job hunting easy. You post a list of jobs you hated, and Monster or CareerBuilder or any number of other sites will try to match you to a similar job that you will probably hate, again. No wonder Millennials only last 13 months in a job. Think about online dating for a moment. If you put 100 percent of your dating efforts into the Internet, you are reducing your options to the people who also put themselves online. Job hunting is much the same. Internet searches should supplement your job search, not be the primary gateway. Imagine if you were matched to a job for perfection, not because it matched past jobs you disliked, but to a job perhaps you'd never thought of because it sings to who you are and what you love to do.

One element of the classic job hunt is true: you should

put at least as much work into looking for a job as you would if you had steady employment. The difference with innovative and creative companies is that they aren't always sure about whom, or when, they need to hire. Which is why you need to be able to put yourself out there and show them all the reasons to hire you.

It is time to turn the job hunt upside-down, literally. Every year *Fast Company* magazine releases an issue featuring the most innovative companies. They may not feature a particular company that you want to work for, but it is a great resource to start your hunt.

Company websites usually have some kind of "careers" page. At the very least, there is an e-mail address somewhere on that website that will direct your inquiries to someone within the company. Many innovative companies are taking part in social media by actively using their Facebook and Twitter pages. Not only is this a good outlet to contact them through, but it will also serve as a great resource to keep tabs on what that company is doing.

With each company you contact, do everything you can to open up a dialogue. If they are interested in answering your questions then they might want to start asking questions about you. What better way is there to get them to learn things about you? Tell them about the real you. Not the resume you hold and hate.

Expand on the dialogue by offering to meet in person. The best way to find work with a great company is to get out to where the company is. Network. Figure out if they are making a presence at a trade show or investor conference. The more people inside the company who you can get to talk about you, the better shot you have when it comes time to hire.

Face time in this age of job hunting is vastly underrated. Casually conversing with someone, on any topic, is a great way to break the ice and get to know what he or she is all about. You never know what random person might be a potential job contact or employer. While a potential employer may be checking out how you react to things he says and how you work in social settings, you can also be judging them on how well they represent their company and what kind of manager you think they would make. Both of these perspectives are lost in the age of online job hunts. Start interviewing people and companies versus them interviewing you. Powerful. Here's a thought: Why not start networking with other people who don't know what they want to do but have great concern for what they like to do? Success stems from these conversations. Example, Person A:"I like to make jewelry, but I don't know how to market myself." Person B: "I love marketing, but nobody will give me a chance since I don't have the credentials." Hello...

Networking Works

One Christmas Day, I was on a flight from Yakima, WA leaving my grandparents house to return home to my Yugo rental car in Phoenix, Arizona. Wearing my Christmas present (a sweatshirt with green and red electronically flashing Christmas lights), and carrying a hot apple pie in a paper bag with a pint of vodka, I was questioned by a very beautiful Italian man sitting next to me on the plane as to why I was dressed in such a funny costume. I informed him I used to wear suits and drive German cars but now my mission was to look homeless and feed the poor with my grandmother's wonderful apple pies.

The vodka was from grandma for long layovers in Seattle due to the fact that I am at least one-twentieth Russian and a quarter German and need to act the part (for the record, I have two distinctly different grandmothers, the Catholic one and the one who ensures I have enough vodka in my diet).

For some reason my story intrigued the Italian, and he introduced me to one of his friends in Phoenix who assisted in merging Lockheed and Martin, and was at that time a brilliant turn-around specialist. Within a month, I was hired as an interim CEO for this man's company making $120,000 base per year and 48 percent of the profits of any idea I generated or created. The only problem was that I was to focus on aviation and global trade. I knew nothing about the industry, and I cared little about it. However, it was a fairly simple way for me to acquire another Porsche in a relatively short period of time so I accepted the challenge.

My days consisted of being transported by limo for $600 lunch and dinner meetings with global aviation executives. My subordinates, who were 20 years older and far brighter than I, were amused with my stamina but shocked at my ignorance of the industry. I was prideful and let nothing step in my way, including my ignorance. Again, my childlike qualities shone through; qualities that made me appear invincible to others.

If you think you're hot — you're typically hot. I bought my Porsche within 90 days of the appointment and my goal was satisfied, but again I was bored. In my opinion, the aviation industry was filled with a bunch of dry men lacking personality. It's really not suitable to act like a clown while running an airline; however Herb Kelleher (founder of Southwest Airlines), managed to get away with it and become quite successful in doing so. I may have stayed if I could have worked with Herb. Going to air shows was fun because once in a while the pilots would let me crawl around in the cockpit and push buttons in the planes for fun...until I started pushing things I shouldn't, then I got dirty looks. I learned why 15 years later when I ventured on to get my pilot's license. Some things just shouldn't be touched before take-off.

To many, my new job would be a dream come true. But I was bored, so in my free time I focused on changing American burial methodologies using the traditions of the ancient Egyptians (with Betty — from the introduction of this book). The Pharaohs didn't fly mummies; thus I was not interested in aviation. I later spoke to the gentleman who hired me about this idea, and he loved it (I won't explain the concept here or it will cease your reading of the rest of the book). Unfortunately, he thought the idea was very creepy and could not fund such an endeavor. I resigned the next day for multiple reasons, but the first and foremost was that I didn't have a passion for the aviation industry. I sold my Porsche and borrowed my grandmother's 1959 Chevy for transportation until I could figure something else out. I was happy with basically nothing: no job and a classic car that was really cool. I had an idle mind that was ready to go.

My talents were worthless in the stock market decline, and I didn't have any money to start anything new, so I returned to school for a doctorate to specialize in fraud. It seemed appropriate thinking back to my hairball-selling days (which will come later), and trading floor experiences. I wrote and finished the first doctoral dissertation on the Sarbanes-Oxley Act, which kept me content and busy for a moment.

The Sarbanes-Oxley Act is an utterly boring topic matter, so my mind would occasionally wander while reading sections of the Act. Virtually every public company hated the Sarbanes-Oxley Act, but they were mandated to comply with it due to ridiculous company scandals like those of Enron, Arthur Anderson, and a handful of other organizations. It was a heated area of debate at the time, and I was the alleged first and foremost specialist of the Act. In fact, I would go as far to say I was the only one who read the whole document, including the President of the United States and any person in Congress.

As I gazed out my window contemplating boring Section 404 of the Sarbanes-Oxley Act, I noticed we had a lot of Mormon Crickets in Boise, Idaho. They are very creepy looking bugs with alien antennas and beetle-looking bodies. The great State of Idaho was at a loss as to what to do with these little beasts. They would cover the road in swarms and cause car accidents; cars would slide over the top of them. My strange mind started working again.

One of my closest friends, Mick Sprague, decided to help on the idea. We would trap the crickets in boxes and sell them to children as pets for $19.95. Essentially the plan would be to ship them out of state for a profit. The State of Idaho didn't want them, but perhaps Connecticut needed a few. After a quick Google search, I learned the bugs only live 90 days. We would probably get a lot of returns.

At this point it seemed more logical to start lecturing at the university level in my new area of expertise: White Collar Crime and Fraud with an emphasis on the Sarbanes-Oxley Act.

The moral is that talking to one stranger on a plane led me to a job that helped me attain the vehicle of my dreams again, which lead me back to school, which led me to a teaching career that I love. You never know where a little face time with someone will lead. I don't make a lot of money teaching, but I don't care. I had it before and can't recall any significant value in having more currency than everyone else. My friends may disagree with this statement, simply because I used to pay for everyone else to play with me. A few had to quit their jobs to be on my "fun" team. Nonetheless, being happy is far better than being rich.

Meet People!

Meetup.com is one of the best for locating people who meet over common interests. Find the group of people who share the same interests as you or who have the interests of the field that you want to work in. Go. Make friends, and see where it leads.

When I first moved to Colorado, I needed to find some friends, so I joined a Meetup group called "New to Colorado Outdoors Club." It was a motley crew of people who had recently moved to the area and were looking for excitement. Collectively we decided to enter the "Frozen Dead Guy Race" in Nederland, Colorado for some fun. On a yearly basis, the town celebrates a dead guy who was frozen and moved to Nederland, and due to financial restraints, kept on ice in a garden shed in order to be brought back to life when the technology exists.

The main event of the celebration is a parade through town of decorated caskets with a live person inside and six pallbearers, all carrying this weight while dressed in costumes. Afterward, the teams race the coffins against each other over rugged mountainous terrain, in high altitude, snow and mud. It sounded like a delightful day, and I said I was in.

Our team of seven had to agree upon costumes to wear. One of the new members who recently moved from Florida, Matt Marshall, went into elaborate detail on how he thought we should all wear Depends diapers and pink long johns with pacifiers stuck in our mouths. The person in the casket would act as the Octomom, and we would be the infants (of course we had to tie some extra fake children onto the casket for perfection of the design). The men looked horrified but eventually agreed. Matt's creativity was bizarre and funny. We asked him what he did for a living, and he told us he was an accountant, but he assured us that he hated his real job. The entire room burst out laughing.

Matt is now part of my marketing team for YomoWorld.

At an event like that you might not meet someone who is going to directly hire you or introduce you to his or her company. Instead, you'll meet people who are interested in meeting and getting to know new people. Why not tell these people you are looking to change up your career? Tell them about your Yomo or the career field you are looking to get into. You never know with whom you will wind up in conversation. At the very least, you will meet people who may know other people to hire you. The more people who are aware of your intentions, the more you and your innovative spirit will be amplified. Besides, talking to people will help you refine and focus on your Yomo, which will manifest your dreams.

While the Internet may be somewhat worthless when it comes to the actual job hunt, it can still be a great tool for marketing yourself. Creating a "personal brand" online is a great way to help you focus on your career and put yourself out there. Your brand will also send a cohesive message to anyone who is interested in you.

Brand professionals have a lot of different ideas about what a person should ideally do to attract his or her desired audience. For example, if you want a career in the medical field, then you should post blogs and update your Twitter and Facebook feeds about medical community news and events that you have researched or attended. Whatever you can do to show that you are interested in increasing your knowledge about a particular field shows potential employers that you are dedicated enough to work it on your own time.

However, brand professionals will also tell you to clean up your online presence in any way you can. Remove every slightly incriminating photo, update, friend, or interest from your profiles. Be wary of the language you use in your social media updates. Make sure your blogs are pristine and show off your intelligent, professional side. The key to success in social media is to post what you're passionate about. Bring value to your target audience. It leads to networking in real life.

Your online profiles and interests and everything else should be about one thing: you. If you are dead serious about working for an innovative company, then you need to do the research and see how you can best show off your talents and traits through the Internet.

A Short Side Note on Resumes and Job Descriptions

I think we are going to find that resumes will soon be a thing of the past. They just don't work. According to risk consultants at Kroll Inc. and executive search firm CTPartners up to 71 percent of resumes have false information included on them. We have all been taught at some point that a resume should be a page in length. Really? So, 21-year-olds are adding in every keyword imaginable to make their short career in food service look glamorous, and 50-year-olds are deleting experiences so their resumes match one specific career. Whatever the job description says, we miraculously know how to do it with a little help from our friend elaboration. Can you imagine being in an interview and telling the respective future employer your real strengths and inform them you had no intentions of thinking past 2 PM in the afternoon or before 10 am? If applicants are going to lie why shouldn't employers? Everybody is lying to each other in the world of work.

While there is no conclusive research on inaccurate job descriptions, most companies fail to tell you everything about the job. A study by Kendra Palmer Royer at DePaul University found, "significant differences between the required skills and abilities indicated in the job description and those listed on the job analysis." It seems like some human resources departments pull out the job descriptions written from the early 1800s, which were probably drafted using a feather and liquid ink. I have visions of Thomas Edison drafting a job description for a person to sweep the floor, and deciding "account executive" made the job sound more important. If companies actually wrote accurate job descriptions, and people told companies what they really wanted to do and what kind of work environment they wanted, we might gain some ground on job retention. For now, it's a game of who can trick whom better.

After I graduated from school with a doctoral degree, I applied to work for the US Treasury. My job title was a United States Federal Revenue Officer. Very cool, I thought. The job description said I was to be out of the office 75 percent of my work hours chasing corporate tax evading criminals. In fact, I was told being at my desk was frowned upon. In reality, the job title should have been "Federal Paper Clerk." The amount of paperwork we had to complete to get our jobs done kept us in the office 75 percent of the time, and we were lucky if we got to go outside for lunch.

The year I was hired it supposedly cost over $100,000 to train each one of us (3,000 of us in total for just one hiring year). Over 70 percent of the workforce quit within 24 months. The job description was wrong, and people who wanted to chase bad guys don't want to sit in cubes all day doing paper work. That one year of hiring cost the Treasury over $200 million, simply because of inaccurate job descriptions. It gets worse. Instead of changing the job description, they just kept hiring more and more people every year, only to lose them again the following year. Time for a job description rewrite. Or better yet, why don't we tell employers what we can do for them and create our own jobs that we will love, be productive in, and stay in for a long time.

If a resume is necessary, think about a portfolio instead. A resume tells people who you were; a portfolio, however, is as unique as you are. If you were to look at the resume of someone like Mark Zuckerberg, inventor of Facebook, it would probably be pretty dismal. It would show that he is a college dropout who has pretty much only had one job. On paper, Mark looks pretty flat. But his portfolio is far more impressive. Presenting your accomplishments and goals in a visually stimulating way demonstrates your expertise and passions. This will make you stand out to employers and innovative companies.

Professional bloggers (those who make money from their blog), say the key to running a successful website is to be specific and cater to a niche audience. Everything that goes into that blog has something to do with a very focused area of thought or industry. These are the people who are able to come up with consistent and engaging content that keeps their audience and their advertisers interested and happy. Your portfolio should be very similar. It should be an accumulation of people you've worked with, ideas you helped develop, and the knowledge you have gained on the projects. Fresh, active, and concise – what else could your audience possibly want? I typically don't use a resume when looking for work. I tell select people what I like to do.

If your Yomo represents your future, then your portfolio represents your past and all of the steps you have taken to get to where you are. Not only does it tell potential employers and coworkers what you are capable of doing, it demonstrates how you think and develop solutions. It can also serve as reminder of a project that you want to revitalize. Your portfolio should compliment your Yomo. Where your portfolio gives a picture of your past and present, your Yomo represents your future and what you are looking forward to doing.

Once again, it is time to turn back to the Internet to supplement your job search. Thousands of tools exist online that can help you showcase your talents and accomplishments. Between photo, video and text presentations you can craft an excellent portfolio that will leave any resume in the dust. Show everyone who you are and what you are working towards. If you have been working in a field, don't just show your best and greatest work. Dig back into the archives and show your very first product or result, even if it isn't great. Being able to show what you are capable of now is good, but showing that you have been able to improve on your skills and abilities is great. Then, presenting your goals further shows your desire to improve yourself beyond that. To me, that is the whole package. I'd hire that person. In fact, I don't hire people based upon resumes — I don't even look at them. I don't even care if they have a degree. I look for the right person to get on the bus. Once in a blue moon I'm wrong, but 99% of the time this works.

The key to getting a fun and innovative career with a company is becoming a fun and innovative person. What are you doing to prove that you are consistently thinking outside of the box?

You picked up this book because you were interested in something different. By the end of the book, you should be able to not only think differently and develop a creative and innovative mindset, but also be able to showcase it to the world.

Exercise #8: Invent a Career

Part I:

A Yomo thinks and sees like a child. They attach to a thought simply by meeting a person or seeing something in their environment that looks particularly interesting. This is a significant reason why a Yomo will change over time: A Yomo will meet new people and have new experiences that will constantly change the Yomo's perception of what is fun. Start looking at the world in a different perspective, one in which anything, quite literally, is possible (regressing back to how you thought when you were nine). When you're watching TV, reading, surfing the Internet etc., notice people doing things that look interesting. You may not know what it's called, but write it down. We fail to know certain careers exist simply because they are not offered in school or there is not a category for them on Monster.com. What does your Yomo find particularly amusing right now? What does it want that's fun?

My example: When I was in junior high I wanted to be a news broadcaster because I saw them speak on TV for a brief 30 minutes, simply reading the news. Once I found out they worked 50 hours a week I wanted nothing to do with the job. I like to think fast and hard and then nap. Twenty years later, I was watching Anthony Robbins on TV give a 45-minute talk; it looked like fun. I like to talk and I love to motivate people. I also love to travel and speak. Additionally, this career seemed to fit into my lack of desire to work long hours.

Some careers I didn't know existed, but seem interesting:
Lead integrator: Apparently someone who works with coders and keeps projects on task.
I/O psychologist: The people that make up questions to put our personalities into numbers.

List jobs or careers you find interesting on the following page. If you don't know the proper name, just describe it as best you can.

Part II:

Are there commonalities between the jobs you listed above? What looks fun to your Yomo right now? Don't think of what you think your Yomo will like later. Make a list of fun things that interest you below.

My Yomo wants to:
Innovate
Travel
Speak
Motivate
Educate
Build things that make a lot of money to donate to worthy causes

Learn about the mind and how it works in order to help others
Write in crayons and colored markers for the rest of my life
Help build other people's dreams

List below what looks fun for your Yomo no matter how silly it might seem:

Part III:

Lastly, use the words above to develop a phrase that describes a fun job. Make sure to use current tense (this is different than your "objective" description on your resume).

My example Yomo: The "Career Innovator" (CI) is ambitious and wants to create new realities out of old systems. The CI will create a new reality in how people find jobs. The new reality is a fictitious world called YomoWorld. The CI will help the job seeker create an avatar to creatively draw out the job seeker's individual passion, commitment and desire to be great. Corporations enter YomoWorld to seek like-minded people who align with their respective company cultures. Those with resumes need not apply. Yomos will work with other Yomos as a team to innovate and develop new companies and ideas. Venture capitalists enter YomoWorld to fund these teams of Yomos.

The CI enjoys speaking to audiences of all ages, motivating them to be better in life. The CI loves to travel! The CI is on the front cover of *Fast Company* magazine as a truly innovative person.

Your turn:

Again, take time to review your list and think about it daily.

Chapter 6: Gaining Focus and Being Persistent

"Be faithful to that which exists nowhere but in yourself — and thus make yourself indispensable."

-André Gide

Innovation/Specialization Cycle

I discussed the importance of having an innovative mind in the last chapter. In this chapter, I want to show you ways to focus your ideas so they can become great, and I want to show you the importance of developing a specialty from your innovative mindset. As we have discussed, specializing is important to make us stand out in whatever career we choose. With both innovation and specialty added to your Yomo, there is nothing that can keep you from being who you want to be and living the life you want.

You will need writing utensils and something to write on for this chapter. I prefer markers and walls, but pens and notebooks are also fine.

First, you need to embrace the frenzy of new ideas that you are undoubtedly coming up with as you learn to think innovatively. At minimum, you are strengthening your existing innovative thinking habits. Everything you see may generate a new idea, a new career track, a new business model, a new invention, and/or a new way to make money. Write each and every idea down, or if you think while you drive, tell your ideas to a voice recorder and write them down when you get home. My dream is that everyone who reads this book will be able to come up with ideas that are all over the map. I want all of my readers, my audience, and everyone in YomoWorld to have huge boxes, notebooks and walls full of ideas. This collection of ideas is the first step in what I like to call the Innovation/Specialization cycle. Each step of the cycle is designed to bring your original idea down to a focused one that can be brought into the world and made great.

Put this flurry of ideas in a place where you can always see them. Perhaps leave sticky notes all over your house, tape your notebook pages to your walls, or just leave them by your bed and take time each day to review them. By having your ideas out and available for review, you will think about them, building stronger neural networks, and focus on the best idea. While whittling down your ideas, don't doubt yourself or consider any of the ideas a "bad idea." Remember how masters of their industry never let anyone tell them they had a bad idea? They also never told themselves "This will never work." You need to do the same. There are no bad ideas, just ideas that seem impossible. With the right team and resources, anything is possible.

So how do you whittle down your plethora of ideas to just one? You'll know it when you see it. Is there one idea you just can't shake? An idea you dream about, or talk about constantly? Do you research a particular idea whenever you sit down at a computer? This is the idea in which you need to specialize.

Now that we have taken the time to focus on one specific idea, it is time to go the other way and expand upon it. That's right. First we innovate our thinking and create lots of ideas, then we focus in on one idea to specialize in, then we innovate that idea further, and then specialize it further. See why I call it a cycle? From your one favorite idea, what are you able to create/develop? How many different ways can it become a skill, a business model, or monetized for maximum profit? You may also discover that as you start to focus in on one idea, dozens of other ideas related to it come up. That's great! Write those ideas down. Once again, there are no bad ideas. Write them all out, map them out, see where each aspect of your idea can go.

At this point you might have discovered how easy it is for the innovation/specialization cycle to spin out of control. An idea spawns three more, and they, in turn, have four other ideas each tied to them, until you are looking at a whirlpool of possibilities.

The way you focus an idea is much like the way you develop a strong neural pathway. In fact, one action leads to the other. That is to say, focusing on one idea can set you apart as an expert. But it can and will create multiple connections and branches off the one neural pathway. This happens when you talk with other experts and professionals on the same topic to continue your learning, and it happens when you are able to integrate your new neural pathway with other already established connections. The resulting network of pathways produces something entirely new!

Apple's Steve Jobs took a course in calligraphy after he dropped out of college. His specialty was primarily geared towards software development, but the calligraphy course opened his mind to the idea of aesthetic appreciation. This lead him to the idea of combining well-designed operating systems and beautifully crafted machines, which resulted in the iPod, the MacBook, and the iPads that when first released were unprecedented in capability and quality.

Twitter is another great example of the innovation/specialization cycle. The Twitter developers specialized in communication and then innovated it. The original software was so innovative, the early adopters weren't entirely sure what they were supposed to be doing with it. It was criticized as being "the thing you use to tell people what you had for lunch." When Twitter launched, people were sending, receiving, forwarding, and saving an unprecedented amount of text messages. It wasn't that people had difficulty thinking in 140 character increments — they just had a hard time applying it to communicating to the masses. SMS text messages are 140 characters long and reach one person at a time, and tweets are limited to 140 characters, but reach hundreds or thousands of people at a time. Was this just coincidence? No way.

The inventors of Twitter first contemplated the way we were communicating and then innovated upon it. In the early days of Twitter, you could update your status from the computer or by sending a text message to your account. Twitter engineers started with concepts we were already familiar with: texting, the Internet, and our desire to share our thoughts with other people. Then they innovated those concepts and changed the way we communicate. Since the release of Twitter, other application developers have further innovated the way we communicate by adding Twitter and Facebook share links to almost every website, creating URL shortening websites, and putting Twitter specific applications on our phones, making it easier to communicate with all of our followers. Marketers use it as a tool to sell ideas and products to people. Revolutionaries use it to gather a following to start revolutions and organize the masses against vile dictators. None of this would have been possible if the Twitter inventors hadn't focused on what they wanted to do (allow everyone to communicate with everyone).

As you delve deeper into your specialties, your neural networks talk to each other, eventually, creating crazy, ingenious ideas that have never entered the landscape of thought before. Like a chef who combines flavors or cuisine styles for the first time, you come up with something unprecedented. By focusing on that one idea and strengthening your neural networks, your eyes will open to the resources out there for you. It can be powerful.

Exercise #9: Family Matters

Harvard Business School (HBS) professor Clayton M. Christensen gave a speech to his 2010 graduating class on how to find meaning in life. Christensen's speech had nothing to do with economics, but he asked his students "How will you measure your life?" Christensen tells his eager, brilliant, soon to be HBS graduates not to reserve their best thinking for their careers. Are you curious what some of the brightest in the nation have been taught as far as their thinking is concerned?

On the last day of class, Christensen asked his students three questions: "First, how can I be sure that I'll be happy in my career? Second, how can I be sure that my relationship with my spouse and my family becomes an enduring source of happiness? Third, how can I be sure I'll stay out of jail?" The third question may seem unusual, but it is a valid question. In fact, "Keeping students from enduring prison time" is in the course objectives for my management class that focuses on white-collar crime and fraud. Jeffrey Skilling of Enron was a classmate of Christensen's at Harvard Business School. Mr. Skilling was later sent to the kind of school where they hold class behind bars and everyone wears an orange jumpsuit. It's a different form of Ivy League, and I'm sure Mr. Skilling's parents are quite proud. Even worse, two of the 32 people in Dr. Christensen's Rhodes scholar class have spent time in jail. Not good statistics.

Christensen goes on to say:

"Over the years I've watched the fates of my HBS classmates from 1979 unfold; I've seen more and more of them come to reunions unhappy, divorced, and alienated from their children. I can guarantee you that not a single one of them graduated with the deliberate strategy of getting divorced and raising children who would become estranged from them. And yet a shocking number of them implement that strategy. The reason? They didn't keep the purpose of their lives front and center as they decided how to spend their time, talents, and energy."

I would highly recommend giving this some thought and retrieving Christensen's speech in written format at www.hbr.org: "How Will You Measure Your Life" July-August 2010. Go read it right now before you forget, and don't worry about paying the $6 to retrieve the article — it's worth it.

How will your Yomo balance career and family?

For example, will you split your time 50 percent career/50 percent family? This is a decision very few people consider, and it's one of the reasons we have such a high divorce rate in this country. If you place your career at 85 percent, I am fairly certain you should not get married. In my 20s I placed my career ratio at 100 percent. Knowing this would not be good in a family situation, I decided to remain single.

I am now at the stage in my life when I could reduce the ratio down to a 50/50 split and be quite pleased to do so. Unfortunately being with a serial entrepreneur like me is difficult on a person. I may need to learn how to meditate, stand on my head for 10 minutes a day, or burn incense to calm down before I get into a real relationship. This is something new I will add to my Yomo. I can't see my future spouse being happy about the fact that I sold our house on the weekend over a "great idea" that I had while in the bathtub on Thursday afternoon.

This step is extremely important if you want a family. Don't ruin someone else's life in the pursuit of your own happiness simply because you failed to develop this balance.

This is also a good place to start building the neural networks related to family. Are you single now and want to get married? Are you married, but want to spend all your time working? Plant the neural seeds by writing out your Yomo's desires below and on the following page; don't forget the ratio of career to family time. Do I have to remind you to keep this in your thoughts?

Chapter 7: Specialization and Entrepreneurship

"For the past 33 years, I have looked in the mirror every morning and asked myself: 'If today were the last day of my life, would I want to do what I am about to do today?' And whenever the answer has been 'No' for too many days in a row, I know I need to change something. Remembering that I'll be dead soon is the most important tool I've ever encountered to help me make the big choices in life. Because almost everything — all external expectations, all pride, all fear of embarrassment or failure — these things just fall away in the face of death, leaving only what is truly important. Remembering that you are going to die is the best way I know to avoid the trap of thinking you have something to lose. You are already naked. There is no reason not to follow your heart."

-Steve Jobs

Entrepreneurs are the controllers of the world of invention, innovation, and they understand that the future of everything is built upon the ideas they create and execute. Being an entrepreneur requires more energy, dedication, and effort than you have probably put into anything, ever. But the payoff is a job you are so passionate about that you can't stop thinking about it, learning you have the strength to fail, and the reward of building something. As challenging as starting or joining a new business venture can be, I highly advise everyone to give it at least one honest try. Not only should we all be interested in changing our careers, but we should also have the courage to create our own careers from scratch. If you don't want to start a company, at least look for one that is run by people who have a passion for the concept.

Innovators and entrepreneurs are not considered

"normal." In fact, statistically speaking, the average entrepreneur has over 500 ideas a year. We are the people who can't get our hair cut without coming up with creative ideas about how to bag and sell the hair on the floor. Ooh, I could see it on Craigslist as bunny tails for Halloween costumes. No matter if you have one great idea for a nickel polish that you discovered by accident, or a new idea every ten minutes, everyone is an entrepreneur at some level.

My first entrepreneurial endeavor started at the ripe old age of nine. Remember I told you my first job was selling dreams? Noticing that my dog had far more hair than needed, I proceeded to clip all the excess off him and sold the remnants to the neighborhood children for a quarter. I told my little friends to think about a perfect life and blow on the "magic" hair fluff ball and their dreams would come true. It was a simple repackaging concept.

Unfortunately, my strict Catholic grandmother was displeased with the dog's haircut, determined I had joined the mafia, and promptly made me refund all my profits. I suppose this could be noted as my first business failure as well. My grandmother's demands nearly forced me into a Chapter 7 bankruptcy.

Fortunately, I knew the Catholic Church was loaded, and had visions of requesting a loan from the Pope to start a new endeavor. This is how we think as children. Grandmother set me straight on this thought as well and, of course, informed me that I could do no such thing. My first deprogramming moment. Frustrated, I walked across the street to get an application at the local 7-11 convenience store, but the manager informed me I had to be 18 to apply. Finding nine to be a difficult age, I resorted to the rotten apple resale business — collecting fallen rotten apples from yards for pay and selling them to their apple tree owners' neighbors, who wanted to bake pies. It was fun. I was later grounded for that business endeavor as well, since I came home past my curfew. I could keep my pay this time.

Obviously you may not think quite the same way I do; you may not be a serial entrepreneur. It really doesn't matter what category you fall into. Because all of us are entrepreneurs of some sort. Let me restate the last sentence again: Everyone Is an Entrepreneur. Most people wouldn't look at professional violinists as entrepreneurs, but they are. They have a special talent that very few other people have. They develop their ability through practice and then sell their services to people who do not have the same talent. Likewise, your talents and skills need to be developed by honing in on your primary specialization. Standard thinking will never accomplish this task.

What makes my thinking slightly different is that I have never conformed to the deprogramming process. Back in the day I would have called the Pope if I knew how to, and I still wouldn't hesitate to call him tomorrow if I had a good idea that I thought he needed to know about. That's why we have successful innovators and entrepreneurs today; they simply won't take "No" for an answer. Their childlike mindset over-burdens the opponent with a chain of "Why not?" questions. Eventually the questions become exhausting, and the opponent walks from the game or becomes an ally.

I felt it was important to address starting your own company in this book, as it is probably the best way to showcase how innovative you can be. Many people are successful working with an established company.

Working for a company that makes and sells the widgets of your dreams is great, but why not have your own widget company? Why not figure out a revolutionary way to sell them and manage the company as a competitor?

Every year millions of businesses are started in America. Once started, there are numerous paths the businesses can travel. None of them are particularly easy, all of them present challenges to everyone involved. Many are abandoned or bankrupt within a few years. Some get lucky and are bought out by a larger, more established company. Others are able to sell products or methods to larger companies. Other companies hold strong and manage to raise funding from private investors. Every path is a learning experience, which requires as much innovative thinking as it does business savvy.

One has to be just about demented to invest their entire livelihood into something that could take years to build and, in the end, probably won't work out the way they think it would. In most cases, the chances a business will fail outweigh the chance that they will succeed by a number you might not be comfortable hearing. But, you get to work on something you're passionate about, learn new things, be challenged and inspired, and maybe even be successful. Life is too short to do anything otherwise.

As exciting and limitless as the idea of having your own company may be, I also feel responsible to let you know the risks and realities of hanging your own shingle. In short, be ready to fail several times over. However, be ready to learn from those mistakes for the next company you start as well.

As Seth Godin states in *The Dip*, "I feel like quitting everyday-not all day of course-but I do have my moments." I have my "moments" too, but I have learned how to bust out of them quickly. I highly recommend following Godin's blog on a daily basis. Good man with a lot of insight:

www.SethGodin.com

Specialize to Stand Out

The first thing you need when starting a new endeavor is a good team. Jim Collins, author of Good to Great spent a considerable amount of time analyzing publicly traded companies that had a 15-year upward growth pattern and the leadership within these organizations. Collins found the CEOs had one major trait in common: they knew how to "Get the right people on the bus." The executives informed Collins that it really didn't matter what the job titles were. If you find the right talent, they will figure out how to run things on their own.

Having a collection of people with a wide variety of specialties is how companies like Google and Apple are able to stay on top of their markets. They resolve problems and create brilliant new products because project managers contact people from every area of specialty. Google frequently buys up companies who have been developing a product for years. If they aren't able to do something in-house, they find a company who has already focused on that problem for years. They purchased Grand Central in 2007 in order to bring telephony technology to the Internet. They grew the product out a little more and were able to launch Google Voice in 2009, a service millions use around the world to organize their voicemail and control their phone devices.

Finding specialized people is how I came to own a trading floor. I was just finishing my masters degree and not certain what to do with myself when my old boss (from the mortgage company that I hated), called out of the blue and said, "Hey, you should check out this trading floor in Phoenix."

In the mid-nineties real stock traders paid millions of dollars to acquire a seat to trade stock in New York on the New York Stock Exchange (NYSE). Traders in Phoenix, Arizona seemed unreal. I decided I needed to see this. Sure enough, a new concept had developed. Day trading with high-speed T-1 lines straight into the major exchanges: NYSE and NASDAQ. I looked at this concept for about three minutes and decided to open one in Seattle, WA. Seattle is a trendy, "tech" savvy place, and they needed a remote trading floor.

The next day I booked a flight to New York and then to Dallas, Texas to learn how to build one of these trading floors. They were rather expensive to open: $250,000, and I needed talent that I had yet to acquire in life. I needed traders, licensed people in the securities industries with odd titles such as a Series 7 and 24, a broker dealer, investment, capital, and of course a management team. Clearly I could not do this on my own. I didn't have a quarter of a million dollars, nor did I know how to trade; I wasn't certain what a Series 7/24 person was, and I wondered if a broker dealer sold cocaine to the crazy guys on the floor that wave their hands around all the time.

Within six months I had all of the above (with the exception of the cocaine), including the capital. Obviously, I could not interview from resumes because I didn't know what the positions entailed. I interviewed for personalities. People told me what they could do, and I believed them. I looked for people who spoke to me with great passion about their specialties, and they educated me on the industry. In my pursuit of finding specialists, I even found my birth mother, Candy Lee (I was given up for adoption at birth). Ironically she's a broker dealer in Seattle, a town I had visited prior to opening my firm. She became one of my biggest assets in understanding the industry within a year of meeting, and I was really glad to learn that she did not sell cocaine.

My stepfather, Rocke, is one of the most innovative people I know. He works at Boeing and loves his job. Respectfully they love him because he generates grand ideas for the company, and Boeing will patent his thoughts. It works out for both of them. Rocke has fun creating, and Boeing benefits from his mind. If you are creative, you must find an innovative company to work for, or you will become bored. The only way Boeing has managed to keep Rocke for so long is that they allow him the ability to think outside of the box and run with his fantastic ideas. If I'm not mistaken, Rocke's title is "Super Genius" on his business cards, even though he is a flight test engineer. Close enough. Super genius is far more accurate.

I needed super geniuses in my day trading company, since I didn't know what I was doing. People started to volunteer to work on my project and gave me money to start it. My partners, including the boss that introduced me to online trading, saw my passion to succeed and build a business with quality people. They wanted in and brought money on a very risky investment. Finding people was my only talent at the time, but I was good at locating the right people to jump on board. Using the resume process to build this company would have been like learning Chinese in three days. I looked for people who had specialization and passion. In essence, the people I found taught me how to build the company. That could be you someday. No resumes needed.

Then you need to learn how to utilize your specialists. Like Collins says, I have the ability to attract followers. I am the visionary who says, "Let's go there. Nobody has been there before," and for some reason people feel compelled to follow me like Christopher Columbus. If I was Columbus, and the world was flat, I would literally run the ship over the edge, never to be seen again. You might hear a few "Yippees!" as we approached the edge ready to drop, because I would convince my crew at the last minute that we were all looking for a water roller coaster all along, and the mission was a success. I must say that it is a true talent to be able to get people to follow you into the mysterious and unknown.

My greatest defined fault is having a lack of detail (as discussed prior), and running a close second is being a terrible manager. Luckily, I'm just smart enough to know how to find detailed people who think completely the opposite of me to safeguard the company. I have worn two different shoes in public, worn my eye glasses with one lens missing, and have even worn a skirt inside out for an entire day without noticing. Once, a man asked me on a flight why I had makeup on one eye and not the other. Looking into a mirror, I found that I must have lost interest and started something else before I finished dressing my face. Some of my finer moments I must say.

But it gets worse.

I left a friend in my car to run a quick errand across the street and forgot to use the parking break and/or put the car in gear on a hill. He rolled down the street backwards in the passenger seat with my car. He was visiting from Ireland, so I told him this was an American tradition.

Hold on; I have more:

My father stopped asking me to do anything detailed at the age of 14 after a particularly annoying incident at the airport. Dad was at O'Hare airport in Chicago, which is pretty big, and forgot to see what flight and airline upon which his wife was arriving. He called me from a pay phone and asked me to look on his dresser for the information. I got up from bed and placed him on hold, fixed something to eat, opened the front door, and went back to bed, never to retrieve the information. He couldn't call back either, because the phone was off the hook. Obviously he found her because she is still with him today, but he was pretty upset with me. I simply forgot he was on the phone.

More? Yes. I am a terrible person.

My track coach in junior high literally had to ask me before every race if I had shorts on under my sweats, because during our most important race of the year, I failed to wear my shorts and took my sweats off at the starting line, only to shock everyone in my underwear (at least I was wearing those). I came in dead last because I had to run with my sweats on and hold them up all the way around the track. Needless to say he was mad. I was holding some of the fastest times in the state for sprinting prior to this incident. In a single minute, I lost our team's record because I failed to wear my clothes. Nobody would talk to me afterward, so I stole the school athletics bus while the remaining portion of the competition went on (just drove around in circles). To this day, it's the biggest vehicle I have ever driven. Nobody cared that I was underage driving a state-owned school bus. People just wanted to know why I couldn't remember to wear my clothes on the most important day of the year in athletics for our school.

The stories are endless. I can't fix these things because I'm absent minded and I don't care. I'm never going to change my weaknesses, and I can't read a book that will teach me how to have passion for detail, so there is no point in trying. Better to make a new friend. My talents are not matching shoes or making sure my hair is brushed or managing people, for that matter. I surround myself with people who remind me to wear my skirt the right way and hire people to manage better than I can so I can focus on my talents and passions.

Delegating Your Yomo

While running my trading floor at a solid upward growth cycle for a few years, I learned something very interesting in regards to the art of delegation. After training each department on my own, the managers in these departments would constantly come to me for advice. In year three, I became a "problem-solving tree." My job was to break into the trading markets of China before E-Trade, but instead, I spent my days playing with yellow sticky notes and trying to figure out why computers weren't plugged into the right hole. I once even bought a round trip ticket for my sister (an IT specialist) to fly from Denver to Seattle to fix our printer, since she is an IT geek. She walked into my office, plugged it in, and said, "Let's go to lunch." Clearly, I was losing it, and obviously, E-Trade not only beat me to China, but also in every other place on the face of the earth.

Frustrated with my inability to focus on my visionary abilities, I called a local moving company to relocate my personal office to my home in Queen Anne, WA. I figured my employees could just call with problems, and I could get more accomplished. Nobody called after the first week, and it was at this point I understood I had the right people on the bus; I just needed to get out of their way. They did perfectly fine on their own. I moved out of Washington four months later because the rain started to bug me and flew back to the office once a month. It's liberating to know you're not really as important as you initially thought.

Fail Often, Fail Big

If you decide to innovate, do not fear failure. It's a welcomed guest in the industry.

Venture capitalists (VCs) invest in startups and new ventures to make money in the return on their investment. While every VC has different criteria as to the company they invest in, just about every one of them looks into the people who are running the company. They want to know what their history is, what projects they've worked on before, what they've managed to make successful and, more importantly, what has failed.

Walt Disney, the mind behind the mousy cartoons turned entertainment empire, would not invest in a business venture with his siblings because they wet the bed he shared with them while growing up. He also wouldn't invest in anyone's business unless that person had declared bankruptcy a few times. Odd?

Rumors will always circulate about Disney's sanity and whether or not he is forever suspended in ice. However crazy he may or may not have been (or is), his business practices have been replicated in some ways that are not entirely uncommon. In fact, many investors will only put money into people who have had failed businesses in the past. They want to work with people who know what is at stake, who know what works and what doesn't. Venture capitalists want to work with a person who won't make the same mistakes twice, which means you have to make a mistake to get their attention. Do something to show them that you aren't afraid to take risks, try something unprecedented, and if that fails, take a risk on another idea.

Venture capitalists are business gamblers. They research the startup companies and then use their money to make a bet on whether that company will succeed. If the company makes it, they become a significant shareholder and make a lot of money. If the company doesn't, everyone loses money. Overall, the VCs aren't as much concerned with the magnitude of the idea or the concept of the company, as they are the management team behind it. We have all learned or read that a mentor is great to have. Think of your board as a group of mentors, each with a skill set you don't possess, but value. Most VCs will even tell you that your management team is the single most important factor in building a company. You may have an outstanding business plan, some start-up capital, and a killer product or service, but a VC won't touch your company with a 100-foot pole if they don't think your management team is incredible.

Think about the specialties you have developed or are currently working on. Review your contact list for other people who have specialties and skills that you can work with to create a great team. Think about your portfolio –

if an investor, VC, or even a customer were to look at it today, would they be willing to give you the money you need to bring your business to where you want it?

The principles of the innovation/specialization cycle can also be applied towards developing a new business. Running through that cycle and developing a team to go around it shows that you are not only able to come up with new ideas, but that you are able to execute them as well. Anyone can come up with an idea; few can make something of it.

This is why venture capitalists look for the salesmen who can sell the worst product imaginable. Then they know that it's the person (people), not (necessarily) the product, which they are betting on. After all, anyone can sell a great product. VCs are looking for an impeccable management team with a person who has leadership abilities. Innovation and non-standard thinking are critical. Ironically, they look for people who have worked all hours of the day and night to succeed, but failed. They want to know what you have learned from the experience.

VCs flooded my trading floor in the 90s, and I told them to leave. My company was built with five partners, and we were debt free. We spent a half a million collectively building the firm. Why would I give up 49 percent ownership to have millions of capital dumped in my company to grow bigger?

Answer: E-Trade and Ameritrade took VC money. I was left with a Yugo when tough times hit. You can still buy stock on E-Trade. You would be lucky to find my company on a Google search as a history lesson.

How Bad is Failure?

Bankruptcy is not the end of the world. Declaring that you are bankrupt tells the world that you have taken on more debt than you can reasonably handle. Sure, the things you still owe on are repossessed, and you may never get a reasonable credit card rate ever again, but life does move on. While it is different for a company to declare bankruptcy, the mark on your own record can be just as damaging. However, bankruptcy allows for the path your failed company took to be analyzed to see why things took a turn for the worse. Bad management? Bad market? Faulty product? Having this analysis tied to your name will give future investors a better idea as to what they can expect should they ever decide to invest in you.

You can rest assured that if you want to, you can definitely try again. Sooner or later you will work out all of the kinks to starting a new venture. You will know what to do and, more importantly, what not to do. If you have the guts to risk enough capital for long enough, you might be able to turn the tides and find yourself back on top of the game.

Could You Be a Startup Junky?

There was a brief television program that aired on a specialty network a few years ago called "Startup Junkies." It was about a collection of businessmen who were serial entrepreneurs. During the season, they were attempting to launch a company called Earth Class Mail. The show followed the company from startup to investment and then left the season at a cliffhanger. Sadly, like most startups, the show was canceled halfway through the season.

It may not have been a long running show, but it successfully captured what it was like to work with a startup company. People put in a ridiculous amount of hours, sometimes 80 to 100 hours a week. The program showed how many people seemed jazzed at the idea of working for a startup company, thinking it has some kind of fame or glamour tied to it; then they discovered that most of the people weren't even worth their weight in dirt when it comes time to put in sweat equity. In short, having a startup company as your primary means of income means your life is pretty much chaos.

Every scrap of funding your startup has comes from the last sale you made. Your best foot is always put forward because you have no idea when an "angel investor" could walk through the front door or sit next to you at a bar or in a coffee shop. Competition is everywhere, and they are always trying to knock you out of the running. The government is watching everything you do to make sure not too many laws are broken and that you aren't trying to do anything they aren't already working on in secret. Your kitchen table becomes an office and a conference room. You might start sleeping at your office. Your children might think you are a stranger, and your significant other will more likely than not be upset that they have significantly less attention from you.

If you don't play your hand carefully, the startup lifestyle could very well remove everything else from your life. This is why many startup companies don't get off to a great start. Kids who have come right out of college staff them. They are ideal startup employees because their family obligations are lower and they have a better ability to handle stressful schedules. However, these fresh-faced graduates haven't had quite as many chances to fail.

Mistakes are made, money is ill spent, and shops close within months of opening due to lack of experience.

Being in a startup company is quite a gamble. There is no hourly wage, there is no guaranteed paycheck. You will probably be living entirely off your savings, which never seems to last as long as you expect it to. But it's worth it when you finally succeed.

Of course, you don't have to go full-time into being an entrepreneur. Many people keep a daytime job in order to sustain themselves and their family. These entrepreneurs, however, don't crash into their couches after dinner for an evening of television. Many startups begin out of a side hobby or passion that someone keeps on the sidelines. Nearly every new business gets its start around a kitchen table. New companies rarely lease an office within the first year. Most companies don't lease one at all and set up shop online and invest heavily in online commerce and being able to communicate with clients all over the country.

There are numerous resources available if you are looking to hang your own shingle, if you are just looking to freelance or even build your own company. As ominous as everything has sounded, one thing is abundantly clear: everyone who chooses this path, this way of life, loves it. They do it because they have a passion for something, and they want to take it way beyond the social and cultural norm. They are after the biggest risks because they know it could yield the biggest rewards.

And if you do succeed, big clients and high finance years, maybe someone buys your business, you will probably want to do it again. Your name will be forever tied to being the inventor and innovator behind the company that sold for an amazing amount of money. Other innovative minds and successful business people will want to recruit you to work on their projects. You will get to pick your income, how often you work, where you live, and who you get to interact with. Is there a better definition of freedom?

Think you're up for the task? Are you ready for an experience?

Exercise #10: Make Money Money

Part I:

Yomos need to get paid when they become adults. How will your Yomo get paid when it grows up?

My Yomo will accept the following:

- Percentage of company: Yes
- Ownership: Yes
- Commission: Yes
- Barter System: Yes
- Other (new thoughts offered): Yes
- Internship: Yes
- No pay (just fun, if worthy): Yes
- Hourly: No
- Salary: No

Life in the World of Yomo: 12 Steps to a Perfect Career

List the compensation structures you'll work for here:

Part II: This is the Tricky Part

How much money do you need to make in order to be happy? After you write this number down explain why. For example if you put a million dollars a year, what are you going to do with it? Money can mess with people — that's why a lot of them get stuck in jobs they don't like. Get a vision of what your life would look like in a few years that will make you happy. How much will this lifestyle cost you to maintain?

$_____

For what? Break down this amount:

Remember, if you hate your job but stay for the money, this is the value you place on your happiness. Revisit this number often. Keep it in your mind at all times.

Chapter 8: Persistence

"If you're going to quit, quit before you start."

-Seth Godin

Persistence is vital to everything you do in life. My persistence stems from the need to be challenged and my goal to avoid having a permanent title like Chairman of the BORED. Over the years, I have made several investments and strategic partnerships in great concepts such as children's dinosaur movies, large corporate conferences, mergers and acquisitions for aerospace parts manufacturers, interim CEO positions, management and consulting positions, and a multitude of other concepts and positions. Some worked and some didn't. Persistence is continuing to look for jobs, careers, and activities that make you happy. It is not giving up and settling into one thing forever that you can almost stand just because it pays the bills. That is settling.

For many years, I was confused. I kept thinking there was one thing I would find that I would remain satisfied with forever. At one point I even tried to be normal and acquired that position with the United States Treasury as a Revenue Officer. As I mentioned earlier, the job description said I got to spend most of my time out of the office; I had images of chasing down tax evaders and carrying a gun. Turned out to be mostly a desk job with no guns. I lasted approximately 11 months; I don't think they finished my background check before I left.

Later, I learned there is no such thing as lifelong job satisfaction (not to be confused with satisfaction with people for a lifetime; keep the good ones). Life is meant to change as your mind grows. What we like today may not necessarily be true next year, and that's perfectly fine. Now I understand that persistence is simply a tool to keep life engaging. Do the best you can at whatever you're doing in the moment, but don't settle into something you don't love just because it's comfortable. The minute I start dreading a career, I immediately start looking for an exit strategy. Some might think this is irresponsible, but it's not. If you don't like what you do, then you cannot possibly do it well. Honestly, if you're going to work in a dead end job you can't stand, you might as well move to the end. Find a casket and call yourself good to go. I think they sell them at Costco now, so they must be in high demand.

Persistence goes a long way, but if you forget what your goal is, persistence changes into something called stupidity. Once in my life I failed to follow my Golden Rule of keeping a job I love at all times and found myself working far too long in an organization than I should have.

During my many pursuits, I taught at a large online university for several years. I hated what the school stood for and felt like I was working at a puppy mill. The school was publicly traded so the shareholders were this school's primary concern, not the students. I was also teaching for a large state university at the same time, and my students at the state level university had at least five times the amount of homework as the students in the online university. Even the class was online — I can't be tied down to a lecture hall anymore. It didn't feel right, but when I raised the standard of the class, the school would ask me not to. I felt the online university students were receiving a grave injustice, although they were unaware of it. Apparently, I gained some morals and ethics in my thirties. They often sent me letters reprimanding me. Once I was punished for an assignment on sending my students to the Internet for research:

"Dr. Luke, It has come to our attention that you are requesting your students to research online for their class projects. Some of the sites you have requested that they visit have competing universities advertising with banner ads. We are requesting you cease this process and we will be placing you on another six-month probationary period for this action."

I'm certain a troll who has lived under a mountain for 60 years thought this was a logical request.

I was a rogue teacher in pursuit of raising the educational standard in the school, constantly in trouble and always on probation, but I was one of the most liked by the students. The only redeeming factor was that I taught at a standard higher than the school preferred, and my students regularly thanked me for the service. What student thanks a teacher for having more course work? Oddly enough the school never fired me, and I refused to leave. Once, the school placed a cease and desist order on my class so the students were not allowed to talk to each other online. They were only permitted to do their homework and post assignments. I told the class to blog on the World Wide Web if we couldn't talk in class, and the restriction was lifted in extraordinary time. I was at battle with one of the largest universities in the world, and it was making me miserable, but I loved my students and did not leave.

One afternoon after receiving another complaint from the lovely school administrator, I decided to view a video from Dr. Wayne Dyer about something (I wasn't certain what). In his clip, he said that he had been a tenured professor for a major university, but was not happy. He knew he could do better for society by leaving the educational system and expanding on his own. Years later he was one of the most well known authors in his industry and making millions of dollars.

Dr. Dyer's only fear in quitting his university was that he had a wife and children and did not want to bring them into poverty. At that moment, I remembered my personal mission statement, put the movie on pause, called the school to resign, and started the video again. Although it was a substantial amount of my income at the time, it was the most liberating decision I have made to date. My sister asked how I planned to pay my bills. I told her I was going to be a motivational career speaker; God knows I have had enough experience playing with them. The next day I checked out every book at the library on motivational speaking. Within three weeks, I was on my way to a new career, and I have not looked back since. In other words, I researched the Yomo I wanted to become.

When I told one of my closest friends I quit my job and was going to be a professional speaker, he laughed for three solid minutes with tears falling from his eyes. Eventually, he pulled it together enough to ask, "What are you going to speak about and where? The Gospel of John on a cardboard box in downtown Denver?" I couldn't wait to prove him wrong. Within 10 months, I had accomplished my mission of speaking about careers. There is something thrilling about proving yourself to someone who holds his Ivy League education in high regard. I have since visited half the nation and spoken to thousands of managers and employees, and not once have I used a cardboard box to perch upon to convey my point. The reactions of people at my speeches have been overwhelmingly positive; my persistence has paid off with a new career that I love, and discovery of another great talent that I was unaware of before. It took persistence to find something I enjoy, and to prove the naysayers wrong. With persistence, I found my dream job.

Finding a path to pursue takes a leap of faith. Rarely do we become homeless when we act upon our instincts. Although I hated my job at the online university, it did illuminate for me, through my students' comments and support, that I love the feeling that comes with helping people. It was the neuron, the seed that turned into the maple tree branch through visualization that got me to where I am now — helping people build their careers. I still teach at the university level, but at a very good school. They don't mind if I bust my students' rear ends and most of the students don't mind either. I adore my students and many of them become friends after graduation. I have attended weddings, childbirths, and written hundreds of recommendations for them, and have even appeared in court over a child support issue to keep a student in class. I want them to succeed, and secretly I know it is harder than they think with a very depressing ratio of job satisfaction looming in the forefront.

I completely love my career, but because life is not stagnant I must persistently adapt. After speaking to audiences nationwide, I have come to understand that the great majority of employees, at all levels, in nearly every sector, are dissatisfied with their careers. I surveyed 1,500 respondents in middle management in diverse employment sectors, to learn that job satisfaction ranked a .69 on a scale of 1 to 10 (10 being extreme job happiness). Furthermore, Harvard conducted a study to find that 75 percent of a manager's behavior is replicated in their respective employees.

Recognizing my students, the Millennials, to be the next emerging workgroup in society, I am concerned with the future career paths of my students. If there is a current employment satisfaction ratio in the United States of 6.9 percent, graduating students embarking into the work world will be led by unhappy superiors, who then transmit their unhappiness to the career paths of new workers.

This is when my innovative thinking kicked in again. I connected the plight of our current employees and future employees with how we look for jobs and realized that matching traditional resumes to traditional job descriptions is about as successful for finding desirable jobs as sticking square pegs in round holes. A neural network was created. I began thinking, how can I combine my love of motivational speaking, with my love for Gen Y, and fix the general brokenness of career matching? The Yomo was born. Now, I use my motivational speaking tour to help change the way we think about careers. I help students and corporations create better processes for successful job placement. I help students and corporations identify and encourage entrepreneurial activity. This is what I love to do. It took more than three years to figure it out. I have now been in the industry a decade. Be persistent; do not settle. Do not be standard. It took a multitude of failures to get to this point.

Exercise #11: Foundations and Networks

Ethical Foundations

What would you do for a million dollars? More importantly, what wouldn't you do for that million? Early on in this book, I mentioned that the hourly wage or yearly salary you bring in is how much someone has to pay to tell you what to do, ultimately compromising your happiness.

Where do you draw that line?

Well it's time to draw it, right now. Not just in terms of how little of a paycheck you'd settle for, but what values are you never going to compromise? I will not work on Sundays for religious reasons. What other values do you have? As you draw this line, consider your mission statement. What are you currently doing in your life or job that jeopardizes that statement?

List and describe your Yomo's values below and on the following page:

Support Networks

Support networks are the very things that allow people to get through tough times. Think for a moment about the people who would support your transition into a new career or business. What makes these people stand out in your mind? Who can you rely on? Who will tell you that you can do anything, especially when you doubt yourself? Who would let you crash on their basement couch in case things really go south? If you don't have anyone to list, start your search now.

Ultimately, these will be the people who form your support network. Try not to think of them as a crutch to lean on, but as a safety net to support you if you happen to fail.

List these people on the following page along with why you can rely on them. Remember, support is a two-way street. List what you would be willing to do for them as well:

Chapter 9: In the End, Be Happy

"If you're confused about life, you're not alone. There are almost seven billion of us. That isn't the problem, of course, once you realize that life is neither a problem to be solved nor a game to be won..."
—Matthew B. Crawford

We must constantly listen to what urges us from inside. Constantly. Waking up everyday slightly unhappy is an allergy that can be fixed. Waking up dreading what you do everyday is a heart attack indicator. According to the National Academy of Sciences, chronic stress triggers cell deterioration, increases aging as in muscle weakness and wrinkles, accelerates loss of hearing and eyesight, wreaks havoc on our self-esteem and personal relationships, puts us at risk for alcohol and drug abuse, and shortens our lifespan. You are running on limited time, change needs to be immediate.

The reason I created a Yomo is simple. People can't conceptualize changing themselves, but they can creatively conjure up thoughts of things that are not physically attached to them. For example, how many times have you given people advice on subject matters in which you are not an expert? I have given advice countless times to my friends who have incorrigible children, only to find out later they took my advice to heart and it worked. I don't have any children. I don't know anything about them with the exception that I was one. The solutions we make up often work because of perspective. Those in turmoil often are in too deep to see the answer, but those of us outside the situation see the solutions clearly. This goes for your Yomo. You can implant all your thoughts of perfection, which may seem unattainable to you, into a cartoon character. First, by writing and thinking about this character, and then eventually writing and thinking like this character, one neuron at a time you become the character yourself. The Yomo allows you to think and live in the future while residing in the present. In essence your mind will be two places at once.

The very first step is to simply desire a predetermined feeling. I remember walking into a house for sale when I was 21 years old. The realtor told me the owners were college professors. As I walked around the home it had a really comfortable feeling. There were lots of books and nice rooms with comfortable couches to just sit and contemplate. I remember thinking to myself, "I like this feeling. I want to be a professor someday." That was when the seed was planted, and my path went on course without me even noticing. Success comes to those who are conscious of feeling. Eighteen years later I took the Strengthfinder 2.0 test online. It summarized my strengths and provided a list of recommendations for careers, Teacher and Motivational speaker were at the top of the list. I wonder what it would have said 20 years ago?

Moving forward in life, we find that a great deal of what we learn in school has absolutely nothing to do with a career or even earning a living. One of the world's most leading innovators, Thomas A. Edison, had three months of schooling in total. He didn't need school because he understood the power of thought. He decided what he wanted to know and specialized in it doing his own research and teaching himself stuff that was important to him. Guess who else understood these concepts?

Henry Ford at the age of 16 had a great interest in

mechanics and chose to become an apprentice in a machine shop rather than continue in an academic setting.

William Wrigley Jr., famous for Wrigley chewing gum, had a reputation for being a defiant child and got kicked out of school several times before running away to New York City at the age of eleven. Returning home after three months (he got cold), he was expelled from school once again for throwing a pie at the school's nameplate over the main entrance as a prank.

Orville Wright, prior to inventing the airplane with his brother Wilbur, never graduated from high school. He could be mischievous in the classroom. Following his own interests, rather than the prescribed junior year curriculum, he opted for a series of advanced college preparatory courses. As a result, he was short a few required classes and did not qualify for his high school diploma. So he decided not to attend his last term.

Charles Schwab, namesake of the company, chose to study math and science in school because of an untreated dyslexia. After college and a few miscellaneous jobs, he decided he liked people, was good with numbers, and wanted to own his own business.

John D. Rockefeller learned at the age of 12 that money could work for him. He had saved over $50 earned while working for neighbors and raising turkeys for his mother. He loaned the savings to a local farmer at seven percent interest payable in one year. Rockefeller spent 10 weeks at Folsom's Commercial College, where at 16 years of age, he learned single and double-entry bookkeeping, penmanship, commercial history, mercantile customs, banking, and exchange. His father taught him how to draw up notes and other business papers and the sacredness of contracts. Feeling he had had enough schooling, he applied himself to working.

Dr. Alexander Graham Bell's mother was deaf. The woman he married was also deaf. This influenced the direction of his life. He attended colleges in his hometown of Edinburgh, Scotland, and London and became a professor at Boston University. He followed in his father and grandfather's footsteps, studying elocution (the art of clear speaking). He had been interested in the transmission of sound by electricity for many years before he invented the telephone.

How Do We Become Great and Love Our Jobs?

These men have something in common aside from being hugely successful. They all followed their dreams and learned what they needed in order to make their ideas successful.

When we don't have a clear view of our plan, sometimes college is a good place to start (though, beware of the cost). I always used college as a safe place to hang out when I didn't know what to do with myself, and I don't think I am a rarity. I still attend school for specific degrees I want. I don't need them, but it's now a hobby. I like to learn.

There are very dedicated students who know exactly what they want to do with their degree and jump on board with vigor. I was not one of these people in my 20s. Looking back, I should have been in an entrepreneurial program in college, but I didn't know they existed, I didn't know what the word meant. I majored in what made the most money, and at the time, Public Relations ranked in the top 10 highest paying jobs after college graduation. I didn't know what a public relations major did when I switched my degree, and it didn't matter. I was attending Northern Arizona University, which at the time had one of the best programs in the country for this major, so it made sense. The report I read said people with the degree pulled in 72k a year within three years of graduation. This was way more than doctors and lawyers earned in the early 90s.

After graduating, I took an internship with the office for the Mayor of Phoenix. I learned in school that a Public Relation's graduate makes other people look good in the eye of the public. Working for the Mayor seemed like a great place to start. Within a few months, I learned that I had little desire to promote someone else, and that I would rather promote myself. I lasted six months in this position before deciding to head in a totally new direction.

All successes come from an idea, a seed that you plant in your head, the first neuron of thought on a "thing." At the age of 14, I planted a seed; I was going to wear suits and run a company. In my early 20s, I planted another (granted, one that didn't peek out of the ground), the PR seed. Twenty years later, I added the PR neurons to my motivational speaking neurons and am finally using the skills I learned in my undergraduate program to promote myself. Although we are using Facebook rather than fax these days, the general principles I learned still apply.

The moral of the story is that it doesn't matter what you do in life as long as you enjoy what you're doing in the moment. Pursue the big picture of success and happiness in your head. If you don't know what you want to do when you grow up, it just doesn't matter. The goal is to create a vision of a life that makes you happy. You will get there eventually.

Deadlines

Yomos need deadlines. Once you create a Yomo it is important to start creating dates for the character. This will help you focus and develop networks of neurons quickly. My deadlines are typically a year out, and a few are several years out. Some of my deadlines go decades out, such as my thought about living by the sea surrounded by mountains and teaching full-time at the age of 65. That branch is going to be so fully developed, I may even own a university by then. Who knows? It's critical to look at your Yomo everyday and feel the personality you have built into it. If you develop the Yomo and stick him in your sock drawer, he will fall asleep and nothing will happen. The Yomo is created so you have a constant reminder to never quit. As long as you have the Yomo in front of you, your goal will be accomplished through positive thought. The minute you stop believing in the Yomo, you start breaking down the positive neurons, and consequentially negative ones may start to develop.

Rejoice in Failure

Webster's Dictionary defines failure as "a lack of success." I think that is an improper definition; we should look at failure as a success. You simply cannot walk through life without it, and failure builds character. Remember when I told you venture capitalists don't like to fund entrepreneurial ideas unless the founder has encountered a considerable amount of failure? There is a reason for this: VCs don't want to lose their investment, and they know if you have never failed you definitely will, and they don't want it to happen when their money is backing your idea. We fail at relationships, we make bad decisions, and we typically learn from the experiences. If the failure is painful enough, and we're not idiots, most likely we will try very hard not to do it again. How many times do you need to touch a hot stove before you stop doing such a silly thing?

My failures were not fun, but I know what I did wrong in most cases. In essence, these failures were grand successes. I now know I am a terrible manager and I hate the details of running a company. Now, I go out of my way to find detail-oriented people who think exactly the opposite of me. If someone tries to tell you that you are a failure, respond with this: "Try it. You might like it."

You need to find people who allow you to enhance your natural talents. I even surround myself with friends who are exactly the opposite so I can learn from them, or quite possibly annoy them to death. I once went to a movie with a friend. After purchasing our tickets at the front door, I told him I was going to run to the restroom. He said "No, that's not how we do it." Most people would probably find this comment annoying, but I was excited to see I was with a person so detailed that he had plans on how and when to go to the bathroom. I would never in a million years build a bathroom plan. So, I quickly determined this friend was a "keeper." Years later this person still continues to push me to be a better person by quizzing me and forcing me to think about details. My friend thinks so differently than I do, and I find that refreshing. I also take great comfort in knowing when I do go to the movies, I will never forget the plan and wet my pants. This has never been a problem, but with my lack of detail and age creeping up you never know.

Goals

The exercises included in this book guide you to write down your goals. They help you identify areas of interest and importance that you may not have thought about before. After you finish this book and the exercises, your goals may change and that is OK. I am a fan of writing my top goals down every year. For several decades it was a list, but as my goals have gotten broader my style has changed, but the purpose and outcomes remain the same. First I used specifics, now I describe a picture of what a perfect life looks like with the specifics in present tense even though they have not yet happened. For example, my list started like this years ago:
1. Buy a Porsche
2. Make $300,000 this year
3. Exercise four times a week
4. Find a better person to date

Now my goal looks a bit more like this:
I am a motivational speaker talking to today's youth about the trials and tribulations of careers as we progress through life. I run a large company called YomoWorld.com that networks people to start new companies in the pursuit of finding a career that rocks. I have a very peaceful life, I am married to an awesome man and I am on the cover of *Fast Company* magazine wearing my jeans and a T-shirt (I'm officially over suits). I have donated $15 million to my church and am an extremely active volunteer in the community. I will acquire two children who I named at the age of 12 (not certain how this is going to happen, they may come with their own names). I will have a Border Collie named Lacie and a Great Dane named Martin (after the great Dr. King). I'm certain a cat will be involved from a Walt Disney movie, but it

has yet to be named. Walter sounds interesting. I have a tremendous amount of joy knowing what I do helps people, and fall asleep each night knowing I am on the right career path. And finally, my house is going to look just like the professors home I saw 20 years ago. I live in flip-flops unless it's snowing outside.

Some of this has come to fruition already; the rest will unfold later. Once this is finalized I will build another picture; but the picture will always stay congruent with my mission statement.

I have learned being more specific works better than being general.

The most common reason people fail is because they encounter temporary setbacks and think the mission is impossible. By creating a Yomo with your goals you keep the dream alive. Every time you look at this character it should be a reminder of what you can be and one day you will be. Your Yomo is your list of goals packaged in a cartoon character's suit. When you personally experience defeat and failure look back to the Yomo you have created, and start aspiring all over again.

If you focus on what you can't do or don't know what to do with yourself, that is the place where you will reside. Let's look at what a Yomo would look like if you developed a negative one. Input all the failures you have encountered in life, add as experience all the jobs you've hated, list your weaknesses and maybe the skills you have worked hard to acquire though you don't really like using them. The Yomo is a dismal little creature now, and has no guidance on what career would make you happy. It probably works in a call center and drinks a lot. I have been developing this concept with people nationwide and have only found one person so far that can't see how it will work. The man is a firefighter from Grand Junction, Colorado. He wanted to be a unicorn when he was little and says he still wants to be one now. I thought about gluing a horn on his forehead and taking him for a ride in a Cessna 172.

Again, on a more simplistic level, neural activity does not know the difference between positive or negative thought. If you focus on negative thoughts, you will build negative neural networks. I once heard a professional speaker state that on a daily basis 82 percent of our thoughts are negative. I don't know if this is true, but it would explain why 80 percent of the current workforce is unhappy. Focusing on constructive thoughts is key, and that's why we need to build a Yomo with 100 percent positive thought. In essence a Yomo is your mentor, but it is the ideal of what you will eventually become. We have all heard of the student becoming the teacher, and this is the same concept: the Yomo becomes you, or you become the Yomo. If you start engaging in positive thoughts repetitively, this is what your neurons will magnetize to, one tiny neuron at a time.

This applies throughout your life. Think about retirement. Generally, when we think about retirement, most of us think about our financial status, not what we are going do. On average, most people retire when they are 65 and start collecting social security benefits. Why?! What are they going to do for the next 25 years?! This sounds like an incredibly boring game plan, since so many of us are living into our 90s. I have no plans to retire, ever. If you love what you do why stop at some predetermined age? I plan to go to my grave, computer in hand with a new idea on the screen. I think most people look forward to retirement because they hate their jobs. Try, try, try so hard not to be like this. Plan to wake up proud and strong at the age of 70; create a new dream for that decade, and then another one for your 80s.

For example, I already know what I will be doing at the age of 65 when other people will be retiring. I will be starting my first full time career as a full-time college professor in the country of my choice. I don't know where this country will be, and I don't know what school I will be teaching at or the subject matter; that is not important yet. It will be close to the ocean. Right now, I only teach a class or two a year as an adjunct professor; my primary career is speaking and building companies. The only thing stopping me from this thought would be falling into one of those caskets at Costco before the age of 65. But, I have a plan to take care of myself and will probably drop dead in a lecture hall. The thought is probably a little mortifying for those of you whose grandchildren may be one of in my classes at the moment. The neurons are at work making networks that will make it happen. This is exactly what building a Yomo is about: Think of whatever you want to be and it will happen, from cartoon character to reality.

Life is only limited by your own mind. A Yomo should not be structured with any limiting factors because they are unnecessary. What weaknesses do you currently hold? Let's get those out right now and figure out how you will turn them into strengths. Your weaknesses are someone else's talents. Find those people with talents you lack; they will make you a better person and your weaknesses will disappear. If you see the forest but none of the trees, find someone who sees just the trees. If you see the trees, find a visionary. If you lack social skills find someone who has them, or let someone with social skills find you. If you are a negative person, find someone who is positive and listen to him or her.

People don't know what they are talking about when they tell you how to live your life in mediocrity. The only reason folks tell you things can't be done is because they can't do it themselves. If I were to kidnap you in a plane and drop you off half way around the world with no clothes and no money, the likelihood of you finding your way back home would be pretty great. You would have the desire to get dressed and get home. Unless you have a nasty wife or husband at home, then your desire would drive you to take comfort in staying where I dropped you off. In a year, you might create a completely different life that was more suitable to you simply by being airdropped to a different region. This is what needs to occur in developing a Yomo. Drop the baggage and develop a new you.

The Power of Thought

Have you ever wondered why we use placebos in tests? It's because medical researchers know the mind can do far more than most of us would imagine. We have conducted thousands of tests to prove this point. If a group of people has a problem, such as anxiety, we might give them a pill to calm them. Then give a second group of anxious people a placebo, a sugar pill. Oddly enough many of the folks taking the placebo will have the same reaction as the people taking the actual drug because they think it's doing something to them even though it's not. According to an article in the August 2009 issue of *Wired* magazine, "Yellow pills make the most effective antidepressants, like little doses of pharmaceutical sunshine, red pills can give you a more stimulating kick. The color green reduces anxiety, adding more chill to the pill, and white tablets (particularly those labeled "antacid"), are superior for soothing ulcers, even when they contain nothing but lactose." That is the power of thought at work.

As I stated previously, I am terrible at multiple-choice tests, and I do poorly on all of them. At one point I decided I wanted a private pilot's license, which encompasses flying around in the air for a significant period of time, taking a multiple choice test, and an oral examination with a friendly person from the FAA. Knowing the multiple choice test was going to be a problem for me, I decided to develop a game plan.

The FAA gives you three hours to take the multiple-choice test under camera surveillance (like being locked up in prison). I guess they don't want people flying around in the sky who can't take multiple-choice tests. Every day for a solid month, I visualized my test score as a 94 percent with a completion time of 44 minutes. I had this picture so ingrained in my head that it felt like I had already finished the exam before I even started. I completed the exam in 47 minutes with a 93 percent. Probably the toughest test I have ever taken, and the highest score I have ever received on a multiple choice test. I was so proud of building that neuron branch that I spent an entire day calling and e-mailing everyone I knew to tell them of my accomplishment. Nobody really cared, and the great majority of my friends were just terrified to learn that I would be flying around as a pilot. I think United Airlines went into chapter 11 bankruptcy around this time, and it might be because nobody wanted to fly anymore since they learned who else would be up there with them. An old friend from high school said, "Oh great, now I have to worry about your airplane falling on top of my house because you forgot to put gas in it before you departed."

What's my point? The only way I passed that test with such a high score was through the power of thought. I fix the lack of gas problem by flying with my detail-oriented friend who has the bathroom game plan. He would never leave without gas.

Repetition is critical in building neuron growth. You can't build a Yomo and stop. To become the Yomo in true form you have to think like it constantly. Once you lock in on the desire, the need for repetition, and persistence, the sky is the limit. It doesn't matter what anyone says. There is not a person on this planet that would have thought I could fly a plane or become a doctor. Your brain is on high voltage. Anyone telling you something can't be accomplished may not be. Unless of course you take the person more seriously than your own neurons.

Napoleon Hill quotes an unknown poet in his book *Think and Grow Rich*, which we should all read and understand:

If you think you are beaten, you are,
If you think you dare not, you don't
If you like to win, but you think you can't,
It is almost certain you won't.

If you think you're lost, you're lost
For out of the world we find,
Success begins with a fellow's will-
It's all in the state of mind.

If you think you are outclassed, you are,
You've got to think high to rise,

You've got to be sure of yourself before
You can ever win a prize.

Life's battles don't always go
To the stronger or faster man,
But soon or late the man who wins
Is the man WHO THINKS HE CAN.

Engaging Change

If you're anything like me, your attentions can change with the wind.

We're human, our passions and energies are meant to change. Only robots are designed to do the same thing for all of eternity. Humans have brains and the capacity to change the wiring within those brains to do whatever they desire. It shouldn't be surprising if we want to change what we want to do with our lives. Like the cycle I drew out in chapter six — you do need to focus on a specific idea if you want to prosper.

But what if the ideas are just not working? What if you can see yourself barreling towards a career that isn't what you thought it would be? It makes no sense to pursue something you are not 100 percent interested in doing.

If you find yourself feeling this way, then start over. Throughout this book, I have given you all of the tools you need to refine the process as often as necessary. Frankly, I expect you to restart a time or two. I've restarted plenty of times in my life, when I decided to pursue a new career. I want you to do the same. I want you to think of these activities as jumping off points and brainstorm starters to help you consider every possible outcome your future could have. Start covering your walls with butcher paper. If you don't like what you have created, just hang new paper (even the thought of it slows down or prevents change).

Eliminate the thought that you must know what you need to be for the rest of your life right now. Understand everything you try is a stepping-stone for another stage in your life that will only be greater than the one before. Marvel in the idea that life gets more interesting as you get older. Some people, oddly enough, get better looking. Change is an absolute.

Chapter 10: Putting it All Together

"Mind control is the result of self-discipline and habit. You either control your mind or it controls you."

-Napoleon Hill

By this point it probably feels as though you have made a great deal of progress with developing your dream career. In the previous exercises I have guided you through activities and questions designed to get your intellect flowing and your mind working in a progressive direction. If you have been a diligent and proactive reader, then I expect you to have pages of notes, answers, thoughts, and passages circled with highlighter. I know when I go through a brainstorming session, just looking at all of the notes I created feels like I have accomplished a lot.

However, I haven't. We do not accomplish anything until we start to put the pieces together. To bring up another car analogy: everything you have done so far is the equivalent of collecting the components of a car, but all of the pieces are just lying on your garage floor. There is a chance that some of the pieces don't belong together, that the mutt of a car you're about to assemble won't work because some pieces are measured in English and others are Metric.

How can you tell? By putting one thing together at a time. The engine may look magnificent sitting there, but you have no idea how far that engine will take you until you hook it up to fuel lines, the carburetor, and the rest of the power train. Then we can see how far this mutt of a car can really take us.

My ultimate goal is to make sure you have a vehicle in place to take you on the rest of your journey to a career that you love. All of the activities I had you do have been geared towards getting you in the right mindset to build a Yomo. As I briefly discussed at the very beginning of this journey, your Yomo is the manifestation of everything you want to do with your life and your career. It is the being you want to become.

Step One: the Why and the How

In the second chapter, I discussed the value of having a mission statement, one sentence that serves as a guiding principle to your life, which is entirely unique to you. As the book progressed, you were asked to think about other questions. You hopefully noticed there are places where your mission statement overlaps with other answers. You may have also noticed the mission statement bumps into conflicting ideas.

Before we can go any further, you need to be sure that your mission statement is as solid and grounded. Consider the questions at the end of chapter two again, and see if they still apply to your new mindset.

Of course, why have a mission statement if you don't have the desire or capacity to work towards it? In chapter four, I discussed at length the power of your brain and how, with a little conditioning, you can use it to accomplish just about anything. You will need to have the ability to think differently and build new neural networks quickly and effectively, so you can build and work with your Yomo on a daily basis.

Throughout this book, I have asked you to think about

some pretty grand ideas — getting the job you love, possibly starting a business, the idea of failing, the idea of being the person you always wanted to be — and when you stack them all together, they can feel pretty intimidating. But, remember you are now armed with the power of your thoughts and can develop a great mindset to approach each of those topics.

Remember too, that your thoughts you have can eventually develop into something real and tangible. Thoughts rewire the brain, which changes our habits, which change our futures.

Step Two: Building Your Yomo

The Yomo can be a powerful tool to help you change whatever you want about your life. The Yomo exists as your future self. You should be envious of it; it exists for you to become it. Your ultimate goal is to step into the shoes of the Yomo and think as though you exist as it. This is why it is so important that we think carefully about what our Yomo represents. You should be 100 percent confident in what you put into it or else you could end up in a career that isn't suited for you.

Consider the notes and answers you provided in each of the exercises. Over the next few pages I will be reviewing the questions I asked you earlier. It's time to take what you have been contemplating and translate it into elements that will shape (literally, you will be doing some drawing), your Yomo.

Everything I had you write and think about is how you view it today. What you need to do next is to take those ideas to a grander scale and ask yourself how you want to be years form now. The mission statement, what you define as success, your ability to develop neural networks and work with others — you need to consider all of this in the future tense.

Now is the time to step into the mindset of a child, like I discussed in chapter five, in order to make everything possible. Don't allow any limitations to your thinking or denounce any idea you might have. If you try to build your Yomo as a modern-day adult would — one who has had their mental capacity refined through years of schooling and social norms — then your future will look a lot less bright than it could be.

Close your eyes, and think back to a pleasant memory of your childhood. Think about afternoons in the park, how a playground may as well have been a space station, how the sunshine and the breeze felt. Open up all of your senses to the memory — the smells and the tastes, what you were feeling. Remember how ecstatic and fresh everything seemed? Remember how anything felt possible? That is the kind of mindset you need to be building towards. The only limitations the Yomo knows are the limitations the creator builds into them.

Now, think about each of the answers and ideas you provided to each of the exercises and consider how they apply to your Yomo.

1) Finding My Yomo's Emotions and Qualities
Look at the list of your Yomo's emotions and qualities. Does it make you feel invincible, like a child again? Are you smiling? Does it bring up any other memories? Are there more traits that should be added to the list? This is the emotional personality of your Yomo, and just as our personalities change so can your Yomo. Just be sure it changes for the better.

2) Steal Some Personality

You can't get in trouble for stealing someone's personality. You might catch some flak if you attempt to acquire their entire brand or copy their method of doing things. Everyone's personality is a little bit different, even if you attempt to copy someone. Personalities are developed through a lifetime of experience. Every single thing which happens to us, whether we realize it or not, goes to shape something about our being. There is absolutely no way anyone can steal that from us.

Of course, that doesn't mean you can't acquire particular traits that you like about someone. I do it myself. Whenever I get on a stage, I immediately feel the charismatic traits of Anthony Robbins flow through me. Who better to steal public speaking skills from than the world-renown leader in motivational speaking?

Who do you want to be like? Have you met anyone since you began reading this book that can be added to the list?

3) My Yomo's Mission Statement

If your Yomo is everything you want to become in the future, then shouldn't your Yomo always be living and enjoying whatever it is that you call "success?" This is the only kind of life your Yomo knows — what it is to be successful. Yomos know everything they had to do to get to that point, and they are proud of what they've done. All of these things you will also learn and experience as you progress towards your dream job.

Think about your mission statement for a moment. Is it a statement that you feel you can adhere to for many years? As you start to build the rest of your Yomo, ask yourself if the statement you composed would still adhere to your Yomo and your future self. If it does, great. If not, consider rewriting it a little bit or changing the focus of the statement. While everything doesn't need to match up perfectly, it is easier to accomplish your goals and live the life of the Yomo if you follow the guidance of your statement.

4) Superhero Sized Strengths

Review your list of strengths. Have you found new ones? Are there strengths you wish you had? Add them to the list. Remember your Yomo is your ideal you, and you can do anything and be anyone.

5) My Exceptional Skills

Have you spoken with a coworker, friend or family member lately who has pointed out one of your many skills? Have you given someone advice on something you are or want to be really good at? Have you met someone who is good at something that you aspire to? Add them to your list. How do you feel? Powerful? Unstoppable? Good. You are.

6) Traits to Trash

Now that you know what you don't ever want to do, avoid jobs or careers that require you to do them. If you can't completely avoid them, make new friends who love them and who can do them for you.

7) Work My Yomo Likes

Are there days you love your job? What are you doing on those days? Is there something you did before that you would like to do again? Revisit your list of pleasurable parts of work. If these tasks were part of your everyday life, would you be happy? Would you enjoy going to work?

8) Invent a Career

Hopefully you have been examining the world around you, Googling jobs to find the names of new careers because you saw something cool. If you have found the one you can't stop thinking about, focus on it. If not, keep looking. Keep talking to people; ask them about their work, search the web, your dream job is out there.

9) Family Matters

How's your social life? Now that you have had some time to think more about your ideal career, did you set the ratio correctly between your family and your work life?

10) Make Money Money

Have you revisited your financial goal? Has anything in your life changed indicating a need for an adjustment? What about future changes? Have you planned for emergencies and surprises? Does your preferred method of payment allow for your financial goals?

11) The Line in the Sand

What values does your Yomo have? What lines will you not cross? If it is something you refuse to do, then it is also something your Yomo refuses to do. Drawing a line on certain tasks or career options today will help guide the thinking you put into your Yomo. If your Yomo has no fear of falling into the wrong career somewhere down the line, then you will be able to approach new opportunities with more optimism and confidence.

Congratulations, you've created your Yomo! The Yomo should serve to remind you of everything you are working towards and all of the things you have to do in order to get it. This is your first great step to find a job you love. Your Yomo should be with you very much in the same way your mission statement is — it should be considered and thought about in your day-to-day life.

In a sense, I want you to be envious of your Yomo. I want you to want everything it has.

So, What now?

Step Three: A World Of Yomos

At the beginning of this book I asked you to consider a world where everyone absolutely loves their jobs. Employee satisfaction is at an all time high, jobs are innovative, and the person in each job is the most perfect worker possible for the position. Everyone is happy; everyone is satisfied.

For a short while longer, this particular world will be a fantasy. But, until then, wouldn't it be great if there was a place you could go to meet people who complement your skills and talents, have the perfect job for you or for whom you have the perfect job? That is the exact reason why I am in the process of designing YomoWorld. It seems like a more worthy endeavor than selling Mormon Crickets.

Your Yomo can live in YomoWorld, with all of the other Yomos. It is a place to find and interact with innovative minds just like your own, to collaborate on projects, ideas, jobs and futures. It is also a place where companies can find people who are or will become incredibly valuable employees.

YomoWorld.com will be more than a social networking site; it will go beyond any job search site. Employers and venture capitalists that frequent YomoWorld.com will be looking at the qualities of our Yomo — not at a list of our previous jobs (some of which we didn't even like). They will come to the site looking for people with passion. They won't be looking for just another employee. Instead they'll come to find someone special to be part of something big. These same employers and venture capitalists won't use cleverly worded job descriptions. Players in YomoWorld will team up by innate talents and passions. Employers will team up with the employees who match their company's environment and culture. Finally, we will be wanted for the skills we love and be a part of something big(ger). YomoWorld is a place where opportunities can thrive and where you can find the job you want.

I plan to build this place. In fact, I hope to bump into you somewhere in the digital landscape of YomoWorld.

Exercise #12: Draw Your Yomo

My Yomo is on the title page of this book. Most likely yours will look completely different, but feel free to steal mine if you like it (but don't try to trademark it). Whatever shape or form you create, the actual look of it should make you smile and feel happy. The Yomo I created looks half like the crazy cat I owned for 20 years and simply adored, and half like a fat, green panda bear wearing a crown with horns. I just liked the look of it. Its form is nothing in particular, but it holds all the characteristics of my perfect "thing." Did I tell you I plan to be perfect? I will let you know when that happens. Whenever I look at it, I am reminded of my ideal personality traits, strengths, skills, mission statement, work likes and dislikes, family and money decisions, values, and networks, etc.

Life in the World of Yomo: 12 Steps to a Perfect Career

Draw yours here:

The 45-Day Challenge

Creating a Yomo is easy; however morphing yourself into the avatar is a little more difficult. Try running through the 12 exercises presented in this book everyday for 45 days. Each day you visualize the Yomo and its respective qualities, you will become one step closer to building a larger neurological network in the pursuit for the career path that you desire. Before you get out of bed, run a visual scenario of what a perfect day is going to look like. Feel the emotions. Change will gradually occur, unless of course you built a dysfunctional Yomo, and then you will need to start over again. Start the 45-day challenge today. Mark the date on your calendar and run the process through your head as often as possible. Don't stop after 45 days. This is a lifelong endeavor; the 45-day mark is simply enough time for you to see how this works on a small scale. Go big.

Before you file me away with all your other books, I want to tell you about Betty (my tumbleweed selling partner) as promised. She became a stay at home mother with her lovely daughter Ava, whom I have nicknamed Herb. She found the love of her life and helps him generate ideas for his company as well as assisting in building mine. This is the joy of her life — it's her Yomo. Little Herb is the creation of Betty's perfect Yomo. They are probably sticking asparagus up each other's noses and eating pumpkin ice cream at this very moment.

Run forward today young Yomos... Find a career that rocks!

After Note:

Steve Jobs, co-founder of Apple Incorporated ironically passed away on the day I finished this book. Jobs was not only one of the most innovative men of our time, but a person who held creativity and a passion for loving his career at an entirely different level than most people could imagine. Needless to say, I was shocked and deeply disappointed by the news. It is my wish that after reading this book, someone will build a Yomo to replace this legendary icon in the near future. We need great thinkers and innovators like Steve Jobs. Reread this book as many times as needed to build your Yomo, and remember it takes repetition. We can all be great innovators (or work for those who are) as long as the desire to innovate and create exists.

Come play with me in YomoWorld.
Try it. It feels good.